HOPE RENEWED

Real Stories of Triumph

Over Adversity

By Carmen Lascu

HOPE RENEWED

Real Stories of Triumph Over Adversity

Carmen Lascu asserts her moral right to be identified as the author of this work.

All rights reserved. No part of this publication may be reproduced, stored in a retrieval system, or transmitted in any form or by any means, electronic, mechanical, photocopying, recording, or otherwise, without the prior written permission of the author, except for brief quotations in reviews.

Copyright © 2024 by Carmen Lascu

All rights reserved.

Most biblical quotations are from NIV or NKJV.

Several names in this book have been changed to protect their privacy and others were happy to reveal their full name.

HOPE RENEWED

Real Stories of Triumph

Over Adversity

*This book is dedicated to you.
It is no accident that you are reading this book.
God, the Creator of all things, has planned this moment
because He wants to help you.
There is HOPE.*

The people who shared their stories in this book found hope in God. He restored their lives after they faced deep depression, suicidal thoughts, physical and sexual abuse, drug addiction, excessive drinking, abusive marriages, grief, involvement in New Age practices, witchcraft, and demonic oppression.

For more information about the author, visit carmenlascu.co.uk

hello@carmenlascu.co.uk

TABLE OF CONTENTS

TABLE OF CONTENTS 4

ENDORSEMENTS 7

INTRODUCTION 9

CHAPTER 1 - SPIRITUAL WARFARE & DEMONIC OPPRESSION 15

SEXUAL ABUSE LED TO DRUGS, WITCHCRAFT, AND WORSHIPPING SATAN 16

BREAKING FREE: FROM DRUG ADDICTION TO DELIVERANCE 24

JESUS DESTROYED THE WORKS OF THE DEVIL 43

LEAVING BEHIND UFOS AND DEMONIC SHADOWS 48

FROM NEW AGE CONFUSION TO DIVINE HEALING AND RESTORATION 61

CHAPTER 2 – ABUSE & TRAUMA 67

FROM A BROKEN FAMILY TO A LIFE WITH PURPOSE 68

REJECTED BY HIS PARENTS, ACCEPTED BY GOD 89

FROM ABUSE TO HEALING: OVERCOMING EMOTIONAL AND PHYSICAL PAIN 98

DRAWN TO THE LIGHT: FINDING HOPE AFTER TRAUMA 105

STRUGGLING WITH FAITH: FROM ABUSE TO REDEMPTION 110

CHAPTER 3 – ADDICTION & SUBSTANCE ABUSE 116

RESCUED FROM ALCOHOL, DEPRESSION, AND SUICIDAL THOUGHTS 117

FROM THE STREETS TO SALVATION: ESCAPING DRUGS AND GANGS 126

FROM A CRIMINAL DRUG ADDICT TO A SON OF GOD 131

FROM REBELLION AND THEFT TO DIVINE REDEMPTION 139

CHAPTER 4 – SUPERNATURAL ENCOUNTERS WITH GOD 152

FROM SIKHISM TO SALVATION: A JOURNEY OF FAITH AND DIVINE ENCOUNTERS 153

FROM ISLAM TO JESUS. POWERFUL ENCOUNTERS WITH THE LORD 162

FROM DOUBTING GOD TO MOVING IN POWER AND MAKING DISCIPLES OF CHRIST 178

CHAPTER 5 – MIRACULOUS HEALINGS & NEAR-DEATH EXPERIENCES 182

A SECOND CHANCE: SURVIVING A SEVERE CAR ACCIDENT AND FINDING FAITH 183

BEYOND DEATH AND GRIEF: EMBRACING LIFE AFTER LOSS 194

FROM DISABILITY TO STRENGTH: HOW JESUS TRANSFORMED MY LIFE 203

CHAPTER 6 – MENTAL HEALTH & SPIRITUAL STRUGGLES 213

LOVED, FORGIVEN AND BLESSED WITH A BABY .. 214

A CRY FOR HELP CHANGED HIS DESTINY 220

GOD SPOKE WHEN HE WAS AN UNBELIEVER 224

GOD CARES ABOUT YOU AND YOUR BUSINESS 236

HOPE IN JESUS 245

ABOUT THE AUTHOR 254

ACKNOWLEDGEMENTS 256

ENDORSEMENTS

"Revelation 19:10 says that 'the testimony of Jesus is the Spirit of prophecy'. So, when we share what Jesus has done, it's as if we are calling more forth; it's like saying, "Do it again, God." The testimonies in this book carry great power. Carmen has a very pure heart before the Lord. He is using her to encourage regular people, just like you, to walk in the power and authority of Jesus, through love, every day everywhere you go".

C. Scott Gilbert

Firestorm United Ministries,

Virginia Beach, USA

"I never tire of reading stories of lives radically changed by Jesus. This book is packed full of such encounters. As you read these testimonies, my prayer is that you will be freshly inspired to go out and share the Good News of Jesus".

Janet Johnston
Pastoral worker – King's Community Church,
Southampton, UK

"I have known Carmen for several years now. In that time, I have seen her continue to grow as a passionate follower of Jesus, a strong believer in the Word of God, and a lady highly committed to ministering the gospel of Jesus to everyone she can – with an emphasis on the Holy Spirit's leading and physical healing. Her example is inspirational, and I welcome her contribution to the body of Christ in the UK in this season".

Paul van Essen,
Senior Leader - Greater Life Church,
Staines, UK

INTRODUCTION

There comes a moment when you start to wonder if life is more than what you've experienced so far. Depression, stress, and anxiety can take a toll on your health, well-being, and your whole life. Without love and peace, it's difficult to function—socially, mentally, or physically.

Many teachings and techniques promise to help you overcome your problems, but even if they seem right, they often fail to address the root issue: the hurt and pain that still linger deep in your heart. Positive affirmations, when done in vain, won't solve the problem.

True change must happen from within, in your heart. As the saying goes, "As a man thinks in his heart, so is he." There is great truth in that simple phrase, which comes from the Bible.

Thankfully, there is a way out of the challenges you may be facing. God can turn things around for you. I believe this because He loves you and wants to help you. He did it for me, and for all the people who shared their testimonies in this book.

The stories in this book come from people I've met in various circumstances over the years. Looking back, I see how God had a plan long before I began writing. He connected me with each and every one of them. Each person faced real-life problems, similar to what you may experience now: drug addiction, sexual abuse, excessive drinking, abusive relationships, suicidal thoughts, illnesses, parental abuse, witchcraft, and demonic attacks.

Though their problems varied, they all had one thing in common—when they were in the midst of their storms, they couldn't see a way out. But everything changed when they allowed Jesus to help them. They found the light, and today, their lives are back on track. Each has been brought out of darkness and into light, living healthy and purposeful lives. There is no greater love than the love of God.

There is hope. I encourage you to read this book with an open heart. I'm still in awe of the miracles God performed in these people's lives.

It doesn't matter how much you've messed up or what you've done. Since Jesus died for all sins, there is nothing that God cannot forgive. There is a way to find love, joy, and peace, and to see your life restored. For this transformation to happen, you must be open to the truth that God loves you and wants to help you.

You didn't open this book by accident. God is using it to reveal His power to transform lives. He can change your life too—nothing is impossible for Him. Consider this moment a wake-up call and start believing in things you cannot see with your natural eyes. The root cause of your problems may run deep, but God wants to uproot them and remove them from your life. He wants to heal your heart.

This book exists because God told me to write it to help people see that there is hope in Jesus and that He has the power to transform lives. He can change your life too, if you're willing to let Him. You may wonder why God would turn His face towards you and help. It's because He loves you so much that over 2,000 years ago, He sent His only Son, Jesus, to pay the price for all the wrong things you've done (the Bible calls them sins). Jesus was crucified and resurrected so you could be forgiven and have a personal relationship with God.

Some may see this as cruel, but I want to tell you that this is what love looks like. God didn't want us to live—now or eternally—separated from Him. So, He made a way to reconcile us to Himself, restoring the relationship He had with humanity before Adam and Eve fell for the serpent's deception.

Every story in this book is a testimony of how lives were changed when people allowed Jesus to take control.

If you're struggling with addiction, depression, or feeling trapped in your circumstances, I believe Jesus can help you. Give Him a chance. You've got nothing to lose. I've seen it many times—because of Jesus' death and resurrection, we can receive God's forgiveness. All we have to do is repent, which means turning away from sin and turning to God. Even if you find it hard to stop doing what you know is wrong, that's okay. Jesus will welcome you with open arms and set you free.

You weren't an accident. God created and chose you; He wanted you to be born. God loves you and has a wonderful plan for your life. He sees you as wonderfully made, worthy of love, and accepted into His family. The change begins when you give your life to Jesus and allow Him to help you.

As you read this book, I pray *that*

the God of our Lord Jesus Christ, the glorious Father, may give you the Spirit of wisdom and revelation, so that you may know Him better. I pray that the eyes of your heart may be enlightened in order that you may know the hope to which He has called you, the riches of His glorious inheritance in his holy people, and His incomparably great power for us who believe. That power is the same as the mighty strength He exerted when He raised Christ from the dead and seated Him at His right hand in the heavenly realms, far above all rule and authority, power and dominion, and every name that is invoked, not only in the present age but also in the one to come.

Prayer from Ephesians 1:17-21

CHAPTER 1 - SPIRITUAL WARFARE & DEMONIC OPPRESSION

- Sexual Abuse Led to Drugs, Witchcraft, and Worshipping Satan
- Breaking Free: From Drug Addiction to Deliverance
- Jesus Destroyed the Works of the Devil
- Leaving Behind UFOs and Demonic Shadows
- From New Age Confusion to Divine Healing and Restoration

Stand firm in faith, for every battle in spiritual warfare is won not by our strength, but by the power of Christ within us. Demonic oppression may come, but with God, darkness flees, and His light always prevails.

Sexual Abuse Led to Drugs, Witchcraft, and Worshipping Satan

This is a story of transformation from despair to salvation. It belongs to James – today an evangelist and a missionary who escaped from a life of darkness. A traumatic event that happened when at 13 left deep emotional scars, leading to a life of anger, drugs, and the occult. In a moment of desperation, a cry to God sparked a powerful encounter with Jesus, bringing freedom, healing, and true hope.

Everything started at the age of 13 when I was sexually abused by two older guys who followed me into the toilets. It left me confused, upset and angry, not just outwardly but also inwardly.

Mum and dad were believers, and I know they prayed for me daily, but I did not know Jesus.

All I can say is that I made some bad decisions when I was young.

By the time I was 17, I had found myself being very violent towards others. My parents knew something had happened but did not know what I was up to.

After the sexual abuse, I started to get depressed because deep down within me, I felt empty. Some friends introduced me to solvents and drugs, but this did not help. I felt empty and more depressed.

Looking for Power

During that time, I wanted to get involved in witchcraft because of its power. It all started when I saw my friends playing with the Ouija board - I understood the tremendous demonic power of the Ouija board when I saw windows and glass bottles break.

All this time, I was searching for something. I was looking for the real truth that I could anchor my life on and be able to walk in power. I tried to find my identity on the Ouija board, but I found myself spiralling into depression.

I turned to devil-worshipping after feeling empty with the Ouija board. I said to Satan, "I give you my life, my all, my emotions, my thoughts, my heart and my soul. You can have all of me".

I worshipped Satan regularly. I remember I would go into my bedroom and begin to worship him. I bought books on Satanism and studied the life of a Satanist. Despite doing this, I felt even more empty than I did before.

Seeing that worshipping Satan did not help but it made me feel worse, I became interested in becoming a witch, thinking that this could be the answer.

I heard many stories about witches, and the practice of being a witch looked attractive to me, so I started searching for how to do this.

During this time, I started hearing voices telling me to kill myself. I had suicidal thoughts to the degree that one night I took a long sharp knife and held it against my wrist. I could not do it, but I screamed out, "if you are real, God, show yourself to me". Deep down, I felt I had come to the end of myself.

I was still searching for the truth, and no matter what I tried, I did not find it.

Heaven and Hell Became Real

After that day, I had three spiritual experiences within a month, which revealed Jesus to me.

In my **first experience**, I felt dragged through these gates, down a dark tunnel, and thrown into a cell. While this was happening, I heard people screaming for help. I felt such fear that I shouted 'JESUS'.

Suddenly I was taken up to another gate, but this time it was different. I saw the gate slightly open, and

I could see a crystal-clear river and luscious green grass. I felt waves of peace and waves of joy wash through me. Then I woke up feeling confused about what I dreamt.

The second dream happened a few days later. In the dream, I saw myself laid out on the floor, and I could see stairs coming from above. I started to see people walking down and up the stairs. When I saw the last person, he stopped and looked at me and said, "Your first part of your first dream is part of your eternal destiny".

I belted out of bed, totally shaken by this dream. I did not know what to do.

A few days later, I spoke to a friend who invited me to a gospel meeting. This was the **third experience** that led me to Jesus.

I went to the gospel meeting, and the preacher explained that God so loved the world that He sent His only Son, for whoever believes in Him shall not perish but have everlasting life. This truth got deeply rooted in my heart. The preacher went on to say that Jesus said, *"I am the Way and the Truth and the Life"* (John 14:6). When I heard this, my heart connected, and I realised that I was not just looking for truth and life, I was looking for Jesus. I wanted to know Jesus as the WAY and the TRUTH and the LIFE.

The preacher continued explaining how Jesus took up our pain and suffering and how He was pierced with nails for our sinful nature. He was crushed under the weight of our sinful nature. He also said that the punishment that Jesus took upon himself brought us peace, and by his wounds, we are healed.

As the guy explained about the sufferings Jesus went through, I felt the pain Jesus might have gone through. At this point, I fell to my knees and cried out, "Jesus, you can have all of me". Instantly, my violence began to subside, and within weeks, I became a man of peace.

Instantly, the power of God destroyed

- the addiction to drugs, and now I stand before you as a free man;

- the power of the witchcraft, and now I walk in real truth;

- the suicidal thoughts, and now my mind is renewed in Him.

Today I am a man who is free from the past. I am now walking in real Truth and Power.

I do not know where this lands in your life but when you understand what God has done for me, believe He can do it for you too.

I had to choose to say YES to Jesus; likewise, you have the option to say YES to Him. The Bible declares – "Today is the day of Salvation". This is your day of Salvation. So, if you choose to say YES to Jesus, say this prayer - *"Jesus, I know that I haven't been walking with You. I give You my heart, my life, my all to You, and I receive Your love, Your power, and eternal life. I choose to walk in Your way. I choose to walk in Your truth and the life You have for me".*

If you said that prayer, I would like to welcome you into the Kingdom of God.

Jesus answered, "I am the way and the truth and the life. No one comes to the Father except through me".

John 14:6

James Parkins is part of the senior leadership team as an evangelist which involves local outreaches, national outreaches & international Gospel missions. He is part of Revival Church Bracknell and Hope for Nations International Ministries. You can connect with him through Facebook.

Breaking Free: From Drug Addiction to Deliverance

Chantal's life was filled with turmoil and rebellion despite being raised in a Christian home. Searching for escape through drugs, sex, and occult practises, she felt lost. But even in her darkest moments, God pursued her. A powerful encounter with Jesus ultimately led her to freedom and hope, transforming her life.

Even though I was born into a Christian family, my family life was very turbulent. My parents had a miserable marriage, and divorce was always expected since I could remember.

My father loved Jesus, but my mother was not on the same page. She had severe mental health problems.

My father tried to hide from her attacks and rages, and so he threw himself into his work as a teacher with physically disabled children and later deaf education.

I grew up insecure, confused, and angry.

We went to church every Sunday, but it was more of a rule than anything else, and I found Christianity was legalistic. I rarely saw evidence of love and faith in our daily lives. It seemed more like a lot of rules than anything else. I had never heard of grace when I was growing up, even though my father did family devotions as often as he could, teaching us the Bible... it seemed dead and lifeless.

At six years old, I have a strong memory of my sister and me fighting and my father taking me upon his knee and telling me about Jesus. I remember him explaining that if I asked Jesus to come and live in my heart, He would help me not to fight with her. I wanted this so badly, and it was a moment I will never forget when I said this prayer.

My mother said she was a Christian, but I never saw her having a relationship with Jesus. She kept herself busy with three jobs every day, working till late and so we did not see much of her, but when we did, it was hard. She was often incredibly stressed, angry and violent towards us.

I had a grandmother who loved Jesus. Even though she did not live close by, she bought me some Psalty praise tapes. As a child, I used to put them on in my room, and as I sang along, I would feel this beautiful peace and sense of love fill my room.

At this point, I started talking to Jesus on my long walk home from school. I would find myself singing to Him and telling Him everything.

At age 9, I went to a Christian holiday day camp and here I was baptised in the Holy Spirit and began to talk in tongues.

My older sister and I were sent to boarding school when I was 11. I did not last long there. I felt so depressed that, at some point, I took an overdose of pills to escape from it all. I remember loving the sick feeling of being out of this world. I was floating around for days.

Destructive Life in Boarding School

I started high school in South Africa at age 13 as a day scholar, and my troubles began here. Due to my insecurities, I desperately wanted to fit in. I began to try and join in with the popular groups and do what they did. I started smoking and drinking and getting involved with boys.

Many of the parties I went to were "free for all", so I had to lie to my parents about where I was going, knowing that my parents would never approve.

By age 15, my parents saw my decline and realised I was out of control. They could no longer control me or my actions, so my mother decided I must go to boarding school again. She did not want me at home any longer.

During my first six months of boarding school, I developed anorexia and stopped eating. I became very withdrawn. I had frequent nightmares every night of my mother beating me, and I slept walked most nights around the hostel, waking up in strange places on various nights.

Towards the end of my 16th year, I changed from being quiet and withdrawn to becoming the rebel and bad girl at school. Then started the next two years of bunking out of the hostel most weeknights, hanging out in clubs and bars, smoking dope, and drinking as much as I could, whenever I could.

Eventually, the school hostel politely asked me to leave as they could not control me.

I did, however, manage to finish my A-level exams, and on the day of my last exam, my bags were packed, and I was ready to hit the big world.

Dependent on Drugs

I got a job as a waitress at a restaurant in a big city shortly after this. It was not long before the staff introduced me to the best clubs and designer drugs. And so began my "high and wild life" of drugs and partying, which continued for some years.

The drugs that started as just recreational soon became necessary to survive each day.

Lots of boyfriends came and went. I lived here, there, and everywhere. My weight was dropping significantly. There were many crazy times when I knew I should have died… My life was spinning out of control.

I got arrested for shoplifting, and I made a deal with God. I told Him that if He would get me out of it, I would return to Him.

He did bail me out with no charges, and I kept my end of the deal. I went home and started furiously reading my Bible and going to church. And I experienced His love in such a beautiful way. I would spend long periods in prayer and fasting, seeking Him. I was desperate for God. But the pain in my heart was still there, and it was not long before the drugs lured me back.

My mother was very controlling and wanted me to study and return to the city, which was my downfall. I did not last long in the same city with the same old friends, and soon I returned to my old habits. But the drugs got heavier this time, and the highs got higher. My mental health was suffering too. I dropped out of the course I was studying.

I would have times of wanting to come to Jesus; I had dreams about Him. I heard Him calling me through songs on the radio. I felt Him pursuing me all the time with His love.

In my darkest moments, I felt the Holy Spirit would rise in me, and I would start speaking in tongues. He was still with me. It was what seemed like backward and forward in my faith.

But He never left me. I just could not seem to shake off my demons or the pain of the past.

New Age Follower

I began to have very dark dreams, and in these dreams, I was told to leave behind the beliefs of my childhood. I believed these dreams were correct and began to explore other paths. I became involved with many New Age people and found myself longing for the peace they claimed to have.

I adopted their lifestyle for a season, but my heart longed to connect with the Greatest Spirit on the Earth, the Maker of Heaven and Earth, the One who saw me in my mother's womb, the One whose Son carried my sin, shame and pain. However, I still had the anger, the suffering and the rebellion from my past. I did not want to accept Jesus; I was fighting Him.

Then I had a dream I will never forget. I was meditating and began to levitate around the room, someone walked in and said the Name of Jesus, and I dropped like a stone to the floor. This dream repeated, and I knew quite plainly what it meant. But I still could not surrender and continued more of the high life and all the mess with it.

God Sent Her Future Husband to Save Her

One day I was working in a bar, and a man walked in. He ordered a drink, we chatted, and he took my number. I never thought anything more of it. On the other hand, he was quite astonished that he recognised me from a dream he had. He was on his way to Dubai to a shiny new chef's job in a top hotel while I was continuing my wild life and running from Truth.

About eight months later, I was trapped in a very destructive relationship, and the new drugs I was introduced to meant that addiction had a firm grip on me.

Maintaining such a heavy habit was costly, but it became my world. I struggled to relate to having a normal life like everyone else.

I was losing confidence in myself and became very introverted and fearful.

Then came a text message out of the blue from a number on my phone that said, "Mark Chef in Dubai". He became my lifeline.

At a time when I felt so alone and trapped in my destructive relationship and addiction, here was someone who believed in me.

My parents, divorced by this time, had long since disowned me, and I knew I was an outcast, but Mark spoke words of life to me in each text he sent. He encouraged me and helped me to have confidence again. Because of that, I was able to have the courage to move out and find my place.

Now followed the loneliness, absolute loneliness. I knew God was there, but my life was a mess. I would ask Mark to pray for me on many occasions when I was out of control on a bender of chemicals.

He did not know how to pray, but I told him to ask Jesus to help me. This was the start of Mark's journey to meeting Jesus.

At this time, I got on my knees on the floor in my flat and cried to God, "God, if You are real, will You show yourself to me and get me out of this mess?"

One day, Mark phoned me and shared with me the vision he had for his life, and for the first time in a long time, I felt a shaking of the Holy Spirit. His vision for his life was the same vision God had given me many years ago.

I knew then that I had met my husband. But he was still in Dubai, and I just did not have the strength or ability to get out of my place.

Tormented by Demons

One night, after getting back from an underground party, I saw a picture of a group of witches sitting around a fire, laughing and cackling. The noise of their mocking laughter was so loud in my ears, yet no one else could hear it. From that moment, constant voices started following me wherever I went. Day and night, they mocked, ridiculed, and laughed at me. They were destroying me, and I was full of fear. Everything I did, they watched me, and I became a nervous wreck. I stopped wanting to go out anymore and could hardly leave the house. I was going crazy.

One day I visited an old friend at her parents' house where she was staying, and the strangest thing was that the voices remained behind the fence. They could not come into their property. For the first time in a long time, there was silence. In this family, they were all Christians. As soon as I walked outside, I could hear the voices on the fence again, but they could not come close when I was in their house.

Now I realised what these voices were, and I started understanding the big picture of what was happening. But still, I did not know how to extricate myself from the mess.

Saved by the Grace of God

Eventually, Mark returned from Dubai and got a job at a Game Lodge / Safari Park on the other side of South Africa. He invited me for a week to visit him and, after the week, asked if I would like to stay with him there and eventually get a job at the hotel.

I realised this was my opportunity to come clean and return to Jesus. I had to take this opportunity despite not wanting to leave my life of sin.

Reluctantly, I left my life in the city behind me and began my journey of walking with Jesus again. It was not easy, as the voices were still there, following my every move and thought, but I had got used to them. The fear was still there as well. I had so many strong urges to return to my old lifestyle, but God was having His way now.

I began reading the Bible, knowing that this was what my spirit needed; this was my key to freedom. The more I read from the Bible, the more freedom I began to experience and the more peace I had in my heart. The Word of God fed me and sustained me in the coming months. I clung to God's Word to hold off my addictions. Without His Word, I was lost and empty. I started to teach Mark the Bible every evening when he came home from work. We would sit up till late, with me teaching him all I knew from the Bible. He was so hungry and was born again in a short time as Truth became a revelation for him.

I surrendered my life to Jesus afresh. I baptised Mark in the bath one night, and when he got out, our whole house was immersed in the tangible glory of

God. It was so strong upon us and truly glorious that we could not speak. God was right there in the room with us, and His Heavenly Hosts had filled the room. We were in awe of Him and were speechless in His Great, Holy, and Beautiful Presence. We will never forget this evening.

Attacked by the Devil and Offered to Worship Satan

The devil was angry; he was so unhappy that we turned to Jesus. We began to receive some strange, dark, malicious emails. Someone hacked my phone and listened to my calls.

Satanists began tracking my every move, following us around and playing sick pranks. They would turn off our electricity box outside the house at 9 pm every night and perform strange rituals around the house. We were terrified. We lived in constant fear of what they were going to do next. They broke into our home and smashed the music player so we could no longer play worship music. When we left the lodge once to visit the local town, we would find strange people following us. It was so surreal. I soon discovered that the people from my past - a syndicate which ran drugs, girls, and bouncers, were actually Satanist based, which is how they secured their power. I had never known this. Now they wanted me back.

They knew Mark as he had previously rescued girls from their syndicate, and he had to leave for Dubai to escape their death threats. I had, unknowingly, got involved in these same circles. Now they wanted me back. They made very generous offers to me – to be altar girl in their sacrifices and run the girls in their agencies. There were times when my phone would ring, and I would get recorded podcasts of Anton LaVey, the author of the Satanic Bible. My dreams were bizarre with confrontations between Christians and Satanists.

They did, however, fear me marrying Mark and seemed to think I was their possession and should return to them. They hated him; they wanted me alone. I remember one day we were driving along the motorway when a car came to run us off the road. It was the most terrifying experience I ever had, but as we prayed and cried out to Jesus, we felt angels pushing us ahead of them, and we were able to escape.

The Demons Left

One day I was in our little house praying. The voices were so loud, and I had had enough. I began to pray in tongues, and the tongues grew in authority. I felt righteous anger rise against their mockery and control of me. I felt Jesus' authority in me for the first time since coming back to Christ. The tongues grew louder, and the Holy Spirit more powerful. Suddenly, I heard some loud, high-pitched screaming going off into the distance, which became softer and softer as I continued praying until they were gone and, finally, there was peace and silence.

I knew Mark wanted to marry me, but I was resisting it. For a long time, though, I heard the Holy Spirit telling me that this was my husband. Finally, I could no longer resist the voice of God. I asked him to marry me on Valentine's Day of that leap year, and four days later, we made a covenant with God and each other and got married. We vowed to give our lives for Him and the glory of His Name and use our union to extend His Kingdom and fulfil the vision God gave us many years before.

The satanic syndicate knew immediately about what we did and knew they had lost the battle. Shortly after, we had official documents signed at a local home affairs office.

A New Beginning

The peace I felt was incredible. The fear was gone, and I had such hope for the future. I felt joy deep inside my heart and knew the Maker of Heaven and Earth loves me. His love gave me a reason to live, sing, and surrender my whole life to Him. His Spirit in me made me feel alive. I was a new person as I chose to leave the old behind and embrace the new. I felt like finally my feet were planted on the rock, and I was unshakeable and immovable. I was Jesus' beloved, and He was mine. And so began our journey of walking with Jesus and finding freedom as we fixed our eyes on Him daily.

Therefore, if anyone is in Christ, the new creation has come. The old has gone, the new is here!

2 Corinthians 5:17

Chantal Vorster moves in prophetic ministry. She coordinates prophetic activity across the world, raises up prophets and leads prophetic activation groups. You can find her on Facebook.

Jesus Destroyed the Works of the Devil

Gabrielle was tormented by paranormal activity for much of her life, worsened by her family's use of a Ouija board. Everything changed when she encountered Jesus, finding freedom and peace through His power. Her story is one of deliverance, miraculous healing, and the peace that comes from walking with God.

I have been plagued by paranormal activity for most of my life, starting as a young child. The shadows were not just shadows; they were genuine manifestations of evil coming right up to my face.

My parents played the Ouija board game when I was around nine years old, and by doing this, they opened a pathway to the demons straight to their daughter without them knowing.

The Ouija board became part of my experience as I grew up, and I did not give it much thought. But once my firstborn arrived on the scene, the activity happened more frequently, and it became terrifying to the point that my child was being threatened. Things happened at night and in broad daylight. I have never been able to watch horror movies because it is too close to home, and it brings back memories that I would rather forget.

The spirit world is real, and it has two sides - the bad and the good.

Freedom in Christ

At the age of 37, I joined the right side after God set me up to believe in Jesus. I resisted God for many years, but He knew that to get my attention, He would have to remove me from my busy life. So, He took me on holiday to another country where unbeknown to me, the owner of the holiday home was a bold, energised, Pentecostal female minister. I received the full-on package of sermons and prayer for two weeks in-between sightseeing and having a good time. I needed this as I was a tough nut to crack.

Each day more was revealed to me about who God was and how much He loved me.

The day before I flew home, I gave my heart to the Lord and was immediately filled with the Spirit. All the heaviness I had been carrying for many years was instantly removed. My life changed forever.

God taught me how to clear all the demonic activity out of my life. After I became a Christian, I learned how to use the power of Jesus Christ against evil spirits by praying and declaring the name of Jesus Christ.

It worked; I have never had another paranormal activity experience since then.

Evil spirits are real and can destroy your life. Only God can remove them. I regularly thank Him for protecting my family and me and for giving us the wisdom to live our lives according to the teachings of the Bible.

Miraculous Healing

My second child had severe bowlegs and was referred to a specialist to see what they could do for her. But God miraculously healed her. As a teenager, she experienced God's healing power and saw that God is real.

Better Life with Jesus

Before becoming a Christian, I had been an atheist, not through choice, but because I grew up in an environment where God was not welcome.

For me, the church was just the tradition of performing christenings, weddings, and funerals. At school, religious education was as dull as history (I love history now), so that did not have any effect on me.

My lifestyle had been one of going to parties and getting smashed. As I got to know God, I calmed down significantly and learned that partying was not all that life had to offer. I became more considerate and learned how to forgive all who had done wrong against me. It was not easy, but with time my heart was at peace. The past was left behind me.

There is no Christian who is perfect. I am not perfect, but my life is enriched. I have a relationship with God, who loves me and protects me.

By faith we understand that the universe was formed at God's command, so that what is seen was not made out of what was visible.

Hebrews 11:3

Leaving Behind UFOs and Demonic Shadows

At age 7 (in 1986), James began asking profound questions like "Why are we here?" and "Is there a God?" Driven by curiosity, he started meditating and seeking answers about the universe. This led him on a colourful, yet convoluted journey searching for meaning and divine knowledge, though he initially looked in the wrong places before finding Jesus.

Raised by an atheist father and a spiritual, though non-Christian mother, I occasionally sang Christian hymns in school and even attended Sunday school, but I didn't grasp who Jesus was. My early understanding of the Bible was very universalist and new age in nature. Meanwhile, I had regular supernatural experiences—poltergeist activity, psychic phenomena, and frequent sightings of what I believed were UFOs. Movies like E.T. reinforced my belief in life beyond Earth. My fascination with science, evolution, and the possibility of extraterrestrials further distanced me from traditional Christianity.

Alien Encounters and Spirituality

By age 12, I was convinced that "aliens" had been abducting me since childhood. I confided this to my mother, who responded with, "God will protect you," although I believed the aliens to be far superior to anything divine. While my mother's faith grew stronger, I delved deeper into exploring these beings, dismissing her belief that aliens were demonic as "anti-science." As my encounters continued, I saw Jesus as just another enlightened figure—possibly even extraterrestrial. Meanwhile, my mother integrated herself into the Christian community, while I immersed myself in new age and UFO communities.

By my teens, I was fully immersed in practices like tarot, yoga, mediumship, and even dabbled in darker paths like occultism and devil worship when angry. Alien encounters persisted, and I gained media attention as the UK's youngest abductee at the time, appearing on MTV, The Richard and Judy Show, and several UFO-related documentaries.

I even wrote a memoir, StarCrossed, which was considered by some publishing houses for publication, though it never materialized because of legal issues around my age (though in retrospect I'm glad it didn't!). After all, I passed a forensic polygraph (lie detector) test on The Richard & Judy Show in front of millions of viewers because I was being honest, and yet the veracity of the visitors' message which they transmitted through me was a lie, and so I am glad that was aborted.

Another major source of conflict between me and my mother was my coming out as gay at 16. She lovingly but firmly explained that God made us male and female. I rejected her beliefs as outdated and unscientific, just as I rejected her views on my alien encounters. Pride played a huge role in keeping me away from God. I was convinced that humanity was divine in its own right, what I now see as "the religion of self."

My obsession with UFOs continued, and by 2012, I joined the CE5 movement, where people actively seek contact with extraterrestrials. Dr. Steven Greer's influence helped fuel my belief that these beings were benevolent. I became a leader in the CE5 community, running successful events where we made "contact" with aliens between 2012 and 2021. At the same time, I became more curious about Jesus, fascinated by groups that mentioned His presence during these extraterrestrial encounters, though they considered Him just another ascended master.

Encounter with Jesus

In 2012, despite having no intention of becoming a Christian, I came across the Shroud of Turin and wondered if Jesus might have been a real historical figure. I began focusing on the image of the Shroud during my meditations, reciting Matthew 7:7-8: *"Ask and it will be given to you; seek and you will find; knock and the door will be opened to you."*

After two months of meditative prayer, on July 4th, 2012, I had a life-changing encounter. During prayer, I felt myself being drawn into different realms. Then I heard the voice of Jesus saying, "My Father has many mansions..." I looked up to see His face shimmering, moving between different likenesses. Beams of golden light shone from His face towards me, and I felt a love unlike anything I'd ever experienced — not the detached "oneness" of new age spirituality, but a fiery love, passionate and all-consuming. It was overwhelming and filled me with the fear of the Lord.

This love, I realised, was not just an abstract force; it was personal and sacrificial, as expressed in John 15:13: "Greater love has no one than this: to lay down one's life for one's friends."

This was not the Jesus of my previous encounters—this was the real Jesus. His love was so powerful it felt like it would burn away anything unholy within me. In that moment, He moved into my heart. I felt as though I had been gasping for air, like I had been underwater and could finally breathe again.

Following this encounter, Jesus stayed close to me for weeks. I received confirmations that my experience was genuine. I saw Hebrew letters burning on my forehead, later identified as representing "The Alpha and Omega." A Christian friend helped me see that my experience reflected spiritual baptism as described in Matthew 3:11: "He will baptize you with the Holy Spirit and fire…"

This was the beginning of my journey with Christ, and from that moment, everything changed. Jesus was no longer just another enlightened figure or cosmic being—He was my Savior and Lord.

Unfaithful to Jesus

After my encounter with the Lord, you'd think I would have been sold on faithfulness to Him. But I wasn't ready for sacrifice or change. Instead, I wanted Jesus on my terms, so I ventured into progressive, liberal Christianity, which allowed me to embrace both new age beliefs and my false identity based on same-sex attraction.

However, an unthinkable transformation happened—something only the Holy Spirit could explain. A few factors led to my conversion experience:

1. Awareness of Darkness: During lockdown, I realised evil does exist. This clashed with my previous new-age beliefs that "all is good" or "evil is an illusion." If evil is real, then good

must be too, which aligned with the Christian worldview.

2. Concerns about LGBTQ and Politics: I believed in free will, but I started to question same-sex couples raising children and felt the LGBTQ movement had gone too far. I also became concerned about gender ideology and the need to protect children.

3. Frustration with Woke Culture: The rise of woke-ism, identity politics, and cancel culture also troubled me. I felt there was an attack on traditional values, men, and the family.

4. Moving Towards Cultural Christianity: Influenced by thinkers like Jordan Peterson, I began shifting from my new-age interests to a more moderate, Christian-like position.

5. Red Flags in the UFO Movement: Within CE5 groups, occult practices like Ouija boards and psychedelics became common, and I encountered

individuals dealing with demonic-like possession. These experiences led me to realise that this was not the path I should be on.

Jesus – Stronger than the Evil Spirits

One particularly disturbing event happened around a campfire during a New-age gathering. A man began growling violently, and none of us knew what to do. We felt powerless against this evil. Desperate, I silently called on the name of Jesus, the only one who could conquer sin and evil. The atmosphere changed, and a peaceful presence washed over us. I didn't immediately reveal my prayer, but I knew that it was Jesus who had lifted the darkness.

Faith Is Faithfulness

Shortly afterward, in September 2022, I found myself on my knees, confessing my sins and unfaithfulness to God. I accepted Jesus as my Lord and Savior. I realised that faith isn't just about believing — it's about being faithful in a relationship with Jesus. On that day, I entered into a relationship with Him as my sovereign Lord.

God removed the scales from my eyes, and I gained deep insights:

- The alien encounters I experienced were demonic deceptions. I had been seeking fulfilment in the new-age movement, but it left me spiritually empty.
- I let go of false identities, including the belief that I was "born gay." I accepted my identity as a man made in the image of God.

I saw how the enemy uses our differences, trauma, and confusion to distance us from God.

It was like seeing life through new eyes. Many of the things I had idolized for most of my life were exposed as false, sinful, and contrary to the true God.

Within days of my conversion, I searched for local churches and found one called Horsecastle, an evangelical church with a focus on biblical teaching and fellowship. They've become like a family to me. Since accepting Jesus, the demonic experiences I once faced have ceased. The name of Jesus alone drives them away.

Following Jesus Won't Be Easy, But It Will Be Worth It

I always knew following Jesus wouldn't be easy, which is partly why I resisted for so long. In the progressive and new-age worlds, you could believe and do whatever you wanted—you were effectively your own God. But following Christ is different. As C.S. Lewis said, the Christian story is unexpected, and that makes it all the more likely to be true.

After my conversion, I didn't experience instant freedom. Letting go of decades of false beliefs was painful. The first six months were especially difficult. I would look in the mirror and not recognize myself, feeling like I was losing my mind. But in truth, I was losing my old self. God was renewing my mind, and my heart of stone was becoming a heart of flesh.

Looking back at my former life as a new-ager and alien contactee, I realise that the peace I thought I had was more like a counterfeit high. We constantly talked about "letting go of ego," but it was really all about me—believing what I wanted, doing what felt right, and making no sacrifices. My "self" was god, and the alien visitors were saviour figures. But now, I understand that I am not defined by my self-perception, but by looking to the face of Jesus Christ.

True peace comes from being filled with the Holy Spirit, not from self-empowerment.

Seeing The Face of Christ

"For now we see only a reflection as in a mirror; then we shall see face to face. Now I know in part; then I shall know fully, even as I am fully known." —1 Corinthians 13:12

I hope my testimony inspires you. If you are involved in new-age, CE5, or similar beliefs, I urge you to be open to the Word and the truth of God. Remember who He really is and reclaim your true identity in Christ. His love burns for you, even when you deny Him.

"For God so loved the world that He gave His only begotten Son, that whoever would believe would not perish but have eternal life."

John 3:16

From New Age Confusion to Divine Healing and Restoration

Jennifer's life took a drastic turn when, in her desire to help and heal others, she became entangled in the deceptive allure of New Age practices. Seeking comfort and guidance, she initially trusted mediums and reiki, but these paths led her into a world of spiritual confusion, loss, and brokenness. It wasn't until she encountered the truth of Jesus Christ that she experienced true healing—physically, emotionally, and spiritually. Her remarkable journey from deception to divine restoration is a powerful testimony of faith, transformation, and hope.

Ever since I was little, I always wanted to heal others. I enjoyed loving and helping people. I wanted to be a nurse, but I did not have enough qualifications to do this.

At 19, I fell into what I thought was the loving arms of a medium who shared so much truth about my life that I believed I was directly communicating with God. As I felt so uplifted by the experience, I convinced myself I had direct access to God via him, so I followed him and all his readings. He controlled my life.

At that time, I was urged to live in Cyprus and stay in an abusive marriage. The enemy was destroying me through the demonic world.

I started to break the link and speak to God directly, but then I went to a Mind, Body, and Soul fair where a lady so graciously approached me and said I walked in with angels and she could heal me through reiki for free.

Looking back, after this encounter, I lost my home, job, and car; I lived in a refuge and ended up in a court system. It was terrifying. It is a wonder I am still here!

In October 2019, I went to London to deliver a public speech in Parliament Square on domestic abuse. I felt such heaviness as soon as I stepped off the train. Many people have mentioned the devil, but in New Age, we never discuss this. I was intentionally not asked to speak, so I felt very betrayed.

Then I went to McDonald's with the group I was with, and a lady, high on drugs, collapsed right in front of me in her dressing gown. I watched others continue to eat their food as if she was not there.

The paramedics arrived after the lady collapsed and asked her to wake up as people were eating. I asked loudly, "What type of society have we become where we can eat when a lady is dying before us?" I wanted to hold her, heal her, and remove the people's ignorance about her pain, but I could not do anything.

Then I returned home, and soon after that, two people who, even though they had endured persecution, walked our Earth with grace, forgiveness, and devotion to God and Jesus, told me that New Age was demonic. They also urged me to read the Bible.

Soon after, my amazing sister took me to York, and we stayed in a crisp white apartment. As my home was very colourful, when I returned, I felt a massive need to paint my bedroom white and detach from crystals and all New Age paraphernalia.

A few days later, a beautiful lady sent me The Last Reformation movie. I watched it, repented, got baptised, and received the Holy Spirit.

A short time after this, I realised the devil had deceived me into false teachings.

Then I began healing on the streets through Jesus. This was all very rapid, and I have never been so happy.

Changed from the Inside Out

My life has transformed entirely. Before my baptism, I had a swearing habit, and immediately afterwards, God's Spirit in me rejected anything unholy, and I stopped swearing. I have become a better person and a better parent. God has taken the thorns out of me, and Jesus has healed a lifetime of trauma.

I had post-traumatic stress disorder (PTSD), but I was healed. My back was crumbling, but Jesus healed my back by aligning my legs, as my right leg was shorter than my left leg.

Because today I have love and compassion, I want to heal the sick through Jesus on the streets of East Yorkshire for the rest of my life.

I am so grateful to know who God is and the salvation Jesus brought to us through His sacrifice. The Holy Spirit guides me, and I am filled with love that bursts my heart open.

I stand in God's truth that the enemy is leading the New Age world – it is sugar-coated to look so inviting, but it attacks the kindest hearts. It is designed to keep you away from our Father God and Jesus.

The lost people matter to God. God saves us so we can assist Him in bringing salvation to others. He transforms us so we can help bring transformation to others. Broken people's lives matter to God.

Peter replied, "Repent and be baptised, every one of you, in the name of Jesus Christ for the forgiveness of your sins. And you will receive the gift of the Holy Spirit".

Acts 2:38

CHAPTER 2 – ABUSE & TRAUMA

- From a Broken Family to a Life With Purpose
- Rejected by His Parents, Accepted by God
- From Abuse to Healing: Overcoming Emotional and Physical Pain
- Drawn to the Light: Finding Hope After Trauma
- Struggling with Faith: From Abuse to Redemption

Your past may carry the weight of abuse and trauma, but it doesn't define your future. Healing begins when you recognize that your scars are a testimony of strength, and each step forward is a victory over the pain.

From a Broken Family to a Life With Purpose

Viviana's childhood was marked by pain and abuse, growing up in a broken family with a violent mother and an absent father. The trauma she experienced left her struggling to understand love and battling depression. Despite these hardships, Viviana's life changed when she found faith in Jesus. Through her journey of healing and restoration, she discovered her true purpose in life. Her powerful testimony is a story of transformation, as she embraced God's love and began to heal her heart, her family, and her future.

When I was about 22 years old, I felt very down mentally and spiritually because I realised I did not know how to love. I was worried about how I would succeed in my relationship with my boyfriend then and how I would make it through this when I did not know how to love. I did not know what love was.

I grew up in a broken family in Argentina, where all I received were complaints and physical abuse. My mum beat me so badly that I once ended up in the hospital. My parents came from broken families, and this is what they carried with them into their new family.

The best decision I took was giving my life to Jesus at 16 years old. Looking back, I see that whenever I walked away from God, He came after me and brought me back on the right path. My journey was not easy. I experienced a lot of anger and abuse when I grew up, which influenced how I lived my life until I turned to God and found love.

Two Generations of Broken Families

I did not grow up in a Christian home, and my parents did not know God. At 14, my mum ran away from her alcoholic dad and a very abusive environment. Soon after, she met my dad and got pregnant with my brother when she was 15. They got married, and they stayed together up to this day. Years later, she reconciled with her parents.

My grandma (my mother's mum) was always involved with witchcraft. I remember she used to heal people with these supernatural powers. My grandad was an alcoholic who abused and molested all his children and grandchildren, including myself.

My dad was not raised by his parents, so he grew up on the streets. He had to work to survive and had his first job in a bakery when he was eight. He did not know what a normal family should be like.

Growing up in a family with two broken people was difficult - a mother who had a traumatic experience with her dad and a father who did not have a mum or a dad near him. I have an older brother, a younger brother, and a sister ten years younger than me.

Physically Abused by Mum

Coming from a broken family, my mum did not know how to handle situations. She had an anger issue. I grew up with an overly aggressive, violent mum who abused me physically and mentally. My mum did not know how to explain things to us; all she knew was to beat us up with everything she had, up to the point of bleeding.

Growing up like this was very scary. I remember I asked my mum to help me with homework, but she got so angry that she took her shoe off and hit me on the head so hard that I was severely injured and bled. I did not understand why my mum was so angry and constantly beating us up, and I did not understand why my dad did not say anything about it. I ended up in the hospital. After that, she made me lie about it because she did not want people to know.

This was everyday life for me. Growing up with an angry mum was hard. My dad never hit us but did not protect us either. He provided for the family but never said any positive words or showed any love to his children. He was there in the house, without saying anything to us – no 'Hello', no 'Happy birthday', absolutely nothing.

My mum and my older brother physically abused me for years. This is all I know about my childhood. The situation between my mum and dad was not good either. My dad was jealous, and my mum always had this temper. They were always fighting in the house.

I remember one day, my dad sat with my brothers and me at the dinner table and asked us who we wanted to live with: him or my mum, because they had decided to split up.

I was so angry with what was going on that I said, "I don't want to go with any of you".

Hope in God

Around that time, God was working behind the scenes. My aunty Stella started to go to a local church and, knowing the problems at my house, she asked her pastor to come to our home. I remember this pastor because he had an accent; I think he was from Brazil. He came to our house and prayed for my mum, and I know something happened at that moment because my mum started crying. Things began to change after that to the point that my parents did not divorce; they stayed together, and soon after, my mum got pregnant with my sister.

We all started going to church, and things were okay for a short time until my mum turned away from God and stopped attending church. I continued going to church and attending teenagers' meetings and youth conferences.

During this time, the abuse continued from my mum and my older brother; he always found reasons to beat me up. I cannot blame him for anything; this is all he knew since this was the family environment.

In all that time, I held on to Romans 12:17-19; "*Do not repay anyone evil for evil. Be careful to do what is right in the eyes of everyone. If it is possible, as far as it depends on you, live at peace with everyone. Do not take revenge, my dear friends, but leave room for God's wrath, for it is written: "It is mine to avenge; I will repay," says the Lord*". I always remembered this verse, and I was saying to myself "No matter what people do to me and how much abuse I receive from people, I am going to leave it in the hands of God. I will let God handle this". I did not want to do anything bad and upset God.

Over the years, I continued going to church, and when I was 16, I decided to get baptised and give my life to Jesus. I did not understand what I was doing or what it would be like, but I knew I had to do it. I remember it was very disappointing because no one from my family came. It was just God and me.

After I got baptised, I ran to look at myself in the mirror to see if something had changed in me physically. Nothing changed physically, but I knew I had made the right decision. Something changed on the inside.

My life after my baptism continued to be challenging. The situation in my house was the same, and the abuse continued. Once my mum beat me so badly that I wanted to leave home.

When I was 18 years old, someone gave me the opportunity to go to work in England. I did not know much about it, but I made a crazy decision to accept it. Looking back, I see that God removed me from the hopeless situation I was in at that moment.

God did things in my life without me realising. He will do the same for you. He will change circumstances or remove you from your situation to help you.

I knew deep down that my mum and dad would not change anytime soon, but God had a good plan for my life and needed to remove me from my broken and abusive family.

Lost in a Foreign Country

When I came to England, I was like a lost sheep. I was lost and lonely. I felt like a big wall hit me. I found myself in a foreign country, not knowing anyone, not knowing the language, and working long hours for little money. I had no friends or family, and the worst part was that I did not receive any support from anyone back home.

One day I met a guy in Staines who knew Spanish, and he invited me to his church. I went there on and off. I realised that God did not stay there in Argentina, He came with me, but I did not have a close relationship with Him.

Because I decided to turn my back on God when I was twenty years old, this made me make bad decisions and make mistakes that I still regret. I thought I could do whatever I wanted here in England. No one was watching me.

I did what I wanted, but this did not make me happy. I was feeling depressed and struggling with relationships and friendships in general. I was struggling mentally, and my life continued going downhill without God.

A year later, I met the man who later became my husband, but this did not help because I did not know how to love him.

Grateful to be a Mum

After six years of being in England, I returned to Argentina, but this time I did not go back on my own the way I came. I went back with the man who became my husband. We decided to get married and have a child. When I had my son, I felt like something had changed. I felt God gave me this amazing boy, exactly as I wanted. I was grateful for this, and in return, I thought I should turn back to Him. In 2011, when my son was six months old, I went back to church. I promised God, "I am going back to church, and I am going to serve you. I don't care if my dad or mum gets mad".

The church was very well organised and had some fantastic groups to support their members. There I felt loved by other people and made some great friends.

After staying in Argentina for three years, due to various circumstances, we decided to go back to England. When we came back to England, the reality was different. I did not have a church, and I did not have any group of Christian friends who would pray for me and support me.

For years I was looking for different churches, seeking what I had back in Argentina, and I could not find it here. I wanted the same presence of God, the same group of friends, and the same things I had before. No matter where I looked, I could not find it here.

Back into Depression

Back in England, I felt I was going downhill again. I remember being in a church and feeling I do not belong here. I did not find my place. I was going to church, but instead of feeling better, I was feeling worse. I had problems in my marriage, and we were doing worse than ever. I felt like nothing was changing, and I was not growing in any way. I felt stuck. We were drowning as a family. I always believed that if God is there, it has to make a difference. If God is present, your life cannot be the same.

My husband did not want to live anymore. The problems were too big for us to handle.

I went to a different church, but it was the same. I continued to feel like I was drowning; I could not live another day. I did not want to wake up anymore; I felt mentally and physically tired. I could not do it anymore. This was at the beginning of 2017.

At that time, I wanted to disappear, to run away. I did not care about my home and my children anymore. All I wanted was not to wake up anymore. I felt frustrated because I struggled, even though I believed in God. I was wondering how people that do not know God do life. I did not see the point of living.

The Holy Spirit Unlocked the Potential

I remember one day, I was on the phone with a friend who had recently moved away, and she asked me a question that changed my life: "Have you received the Holy Spirit?" I did not want to answer because I did not know what she was talking about.

Until that point, I did not think about the Holy Spirit. For me, it was God and Jesus. I never paid attention to the Holy Spirit until that moment. When she asked me, I said, "I don't know".

After that call, daily for about a week, she sent me video teachings about the Holy Spirit. She asked me to watch them and promised she would call me next Saturday to discuss this. I listened to them, and the more I listened, the more confused I got.

I thought, "There is no way I could receive that gift. I don't have enough faith. I am not worthy. I do not deserve it. I don't understand".

Next Saturday, I was at home, and when I saw my phone ringing, I said to myself, "Oh, no. There she is. What am I going to say to her? Do I have to lie? What am I going to say?"

She explained to me more about the Holy Spirit, and then she asked me if I wanted to receive the Holy Spirit. Straight away, I thought to myself, "Oh, no. She is one of those crazy people. Now I will have to lie and pretend that I want to receive the Holy Spirit just to make her feel better".

I will never forget that I felt like something overpowered me the minute she prayed for me. I felt heavy in my body and felt a strong power over me. I was not in control anymore. I was crying out so badly.

Straight away, I started to see things differently. I felt like I was a blind person living life in darkness and suddenly, I began to see that life now has colours. I saw that there was a war between the flesh and the spirit. I started to understand what was going on. The word 'holy' made sense now. Holy Spirit had a shape now. At that moment, I heard a voice (in my head) saying, "I am with you; I am with you". Without realising it, I have heard that voice all through my life since I was a child, saying, "I am with you; I am here".

I was not the same after that Saturday afternoon of 27th July 2017. My life changed completely the moment I received the Holy Spirit. Everything became real. There was no religion anymore. This time I wanted to go back to church on Sunday because I needed it. Jesus became real. I started to understand and see God as a Father and that He is love. I began to fall in love with God. It was so overwhelming. I was so hungry, and I wanted more and more of this Holy Spirit, of His presence. I started going to conferences because I wanted more of God's presence.

I believe Jesus came to restore His people - I am one of them. He is restoring my life and putting all the pieces back together. He gave me a new heart and a new purpose. Today I am no longer alone. I am loved. I do not care what is happening around me because I know God is there with me.

There are still some things I struggle with or do not understand entirely, but I know that if He is there with me, nothing and no one can be against me.

No matter what I face in life, I always hold on to the words of Jesus in Mathew 24:13: *"the one who stands firm to the end will be saved"*.

Lost but Now Found

All I want now is for people to know Jesus to experience His love. Before I realised what Jesus did for me and I received the Holy Spirit, I did not know what love was. Growing up in a broken family with an abusive mum who did not know how to love was difficult. We are working on our relationship to this day.

I learned a few years ago to accept my family and to love them the way they are. I cannot change people, but I believe God can. He can change my family. I pray for mercy for my family, and I know I will see them giving their lives to Jesus. They do not realise how much they need Him, but I know. I will keep praying for my family.

My deepest desire is for people to know Jesus because the minute they know Jesus, they will know love, hope, and peace and have everything they need. It breaks my heart when I see many people out there, even in my workplace, that have been abandoned, who never had a father, who have been neglected by their mum, who have been abused by their parents, and who do life without Jesus. I was one of them before, and I was utterly lost. I struggled in every area of my life and marriage because when you do not have God, you are empty, but when Jesus comes into your life, everything changes. This is my primary purpose – for people to know God.

Love may come in different shapes, but genuine unconditional love comes from Jesus. When you meet Jesus, you meet true love.

If you have the same problem I had and do not know how to love, turn to Jesus. Every day when I go to work, I pray, "Jesus, I want to be more like you. I want to love people as you do, and if I have to close my mouth, I will do it".

I want people to see something of Jesus in my life. I want people to ask me, "What is different about you?" or "What can I do to have what you have?".

I do not have much, but I have the best thing anyone can have – I have salvation; I have Jesus in my life. I do not have to worry about tomorrow because Jesus is in it. He is always with me wherever I go. He was there in my worst moments; He is now and will be in the future. I have no worries now that I have the Holy Spirit inside of me, who helps me every day to be a better mum and wife. He provides for me in different ways. I cannot even describe how faithful He is.

God Has a Better Plan

I do not know where I would be today without Jesus. I want to emphasise 1 Corinthians 2:9 because this will highlight my story and my experience from the minute I encountered God to this day: *"No eye has seen, no ear has heard, and no human mind has conceived, the things God has prepared for those who love him"*.

This touched my heart because God did so many things for me, things I did not even ask for. I came from a broken home, an abusive home, was sexually abused, growing up with anger, but God had better plans for me. I hold on and keep believing there is a better plan for me. God is going to transform into a blessing that the devil intended for harm.

God has many amazing plans for me because I chose to give my life to Jesus one day. I made that decision when I was 16. I got baptised and gave my life to Jesus. Then, the day I received the Holy Spirit changed my relationship with God and the world. I believe that these decisions changed the whole future of my life. My children will not have to struggle with the things I struggled with in the past because God made everything new for me. I am holding on to this promise that God prepared great things for those who love Him.

Jesus continues working in me, my marriage, and my family. He gave me a purpose and is guiding me at every step. I received His love and learnt how to love my husband and children. I went back to finish my studies, and He gave me new dreams and hope for the future.

But the one who stands firm to the end will be saved.

Matthew 24:13

Rejected by His Parents, Accepted by God

Born into a complicated and broken family situation, Jeremy's early years were marked by rejection and abandonment. Adopted and later sent to boarding school, he struggled with feelings of rejection throughout his life. Despite his success in other areas, Jeremy felt an emptiness that led him on a spiritual search. It wasn't until he encountered Jesus that he began to understand true love and acceptance. His journey is one of healing, discovering his identity in Christ, and learning to overcome the scars of the past through faith.

My mum had me after having an adulterous relationship with my father. I was the outcome of that relationship, and my father wanted a divorce from his wife (he was clearly unhappy in his marriage), but she would not play ball. My mum resigned to being on her own during the pregnancy and decided to have me and, presumably, bring me up. Unfortunately, she quickly realised she could not cope with being a single mother as in the early 1950s; this was taboo, so she put me into foster care for two years.

It became increasingly evident that I was a troubled little boy, and social services decided I needed the security of one home, so another family adopted me.

Everything was okay in this new family until my adopted parents had another child, and when I was eleven years old, they sent me to a boarding school.

Rejection has always been a sensitive issue for me. We all need to be loved. People spend their lives looking for love, mostly confused with lust.

The problem is perfect love is hard to find via a human being! I spent most of my life needing to be delivered from rejection and little did I know that the solution was to be found in Jesus Christ.

My initial conversion was the fulfilment of seeking the meaning of life. Nothing tragic had happened in my life to motivate me to seek some comfort. I was carrying around my rejection which was affecting my relationships, but I did not know how to solve that pain.

Life was okay, and I did not look for a crutch. I was married, earning decent money, owned a house, and had a beautiful daughter, and yet I knew there was more to life than what I had experienced so far.

I investigated different "religions", not expecting to find anything. And then, in late 1986, I found the truth. My brother-in-law invited me to join him and his wife at church. I accepted his invitation, not expecting anything. It was at North Baddesley Baptist Church. My background was Church of England high church services, so a Baptist service was different and less formal.

At the church, a visiting preacher was giving the sermon. I cannot remember it entirely, but he talked about the cross and invited the listeners to change their minds and believe in Jesus Christ as God's Son and their Saviour. I responded to that invitation thinking that this was what I had been looking for, though I had little understanding of what it meant. That morning, I decided to follow Jesus and started a long and challenging journey.

My conversion was not dramatic. No vision of Jesus. No tingling in my body. No falling. And yet I knew something had happened.

After Conversion

Despite my conversion, I had found the church service uncomfortable. Everyone seemed to know everyone, and this unsettled me. The rejection was rearing its ugly head. So, the following day I decided to find an Anglican Church to visit and pray to God, asking Him what to do next. At the local church in

Otterbourne, I knelt on the pew and prayed to God that He would show me the next step to take.

Jesus says this: *"You may ask me for anything in my name, and I will do it"* (John 14:14).

Faithful to His Word, God answered my prayer, and within a month, I found myself at a house church, free from all the religious trappings generally associated with a high church. I knew at that moment that Chandlers Ford Christian Fellowship was to be my first spiritual home.

The Later Years

Since 1986 my journey with Jesus has been far from smooth. For twenty-five years after my conversion, I walked without the freedom Jesus had bought me on that wondrous cross two thousand years ago.

I have now learned that what happened back in 1986 was that I was "born again" as Jesus said in John

3, *"Very truly I tell you, no one can see the kingdom of God unless they are born again"*.

What I had not understood was that back in late 1986, the old "me" had died on the cross, along with Jesus, and I had become a new creation (2 Corinthians 5:17). I was perplexed that my thinking did not change much, and my body certainly was not new.

Once I received proper teachings that I am a spirit (created in His image – God is Spirit) with a soul (mind, conscience, feelings, emotions, etc.), and live in a body, it all started to make sense. My spirit had been created new and identical to Jesus; Jesus was now in me, and I was in Him. That sounds weird, I know, but it is true.

Jesus said, *"Then you will know* [understand] *the truth and the truth will set you free" (John 8:32).* I had spent twenty-five years as a born-again Christian, thinking I was a second-class believer because I did not understand what the Word of God was saying to me. That is why the Father sent the Holy Spirit, after the ascension of Jesus Christ, to be our helper, teacher, and comforter.

When you get baptised in the Holy Spirit, He comes and lives inside you. When you ask Him questions, He answers. He also teaches you to understand what God's Word is saying. Without the Holy Spirit, you cannot understand Scripture.

Today, over thirty years later, I am still learning to understand the truth. For every individual, Jesus Christ is the only way to a relationship with our Heavenly Father, our Creator. With the Holy Spirit helping us and teaching us, we are on the right road.

What I have learned is that God is good all the time; this is His nature. God loves us so much that He gave His only begotten Son, that if we believe in Jesus Christ as the Son of God and as our Saviour, we will be saved (John 3:16).

The Good News of Jesus Christ is not complicated. Jesus was punished instead of us, so God is no longer angry with us. Jesus is the bridge to a beautiful relationship with our Creator. The revelation of God's love for us is so important, as it releases us to love ourselves and others. I was looking for that love in 1986 and found it later in Jesus Christ.

The rejection I suffered as a baby took many years to heal, and even today, the scars sometimes surface on a bad day when I momentarily forget what Jesus did for me. Those scars are healing, though, and have been replaced with a deeper understanding of God's love for me.

That revelation of God's love comes when we understand God's Word and believe His many promises to us, promises that He keeps.

I am now secure in the knowledge that I have a Heavenly Father who loves me, accepts me, has forgiven me of my sins, and most importantly, has forgotten them. He ONLY wants to bless me, not harm me, and to give me a hope and a future.

For I know the plans I have for you, declares the Lord, plans to prosper you and not to harm you, plans to give you hope and a future.

Jeremiah 29:11

Jeremy Newbegin is the founder of Grace and Faith Ministries (graceandfaithministries.co.uk); he teaches the Word of God and have been called to help set up a school in Kenya for orphans and children from poor families.

From Abuse to Healing: Overcoming Emotional and Physical Pain

Raised in a religious environment without truly knowing God, Patricia found peace and healing after surrendering her life to Jesus. From overcoming an autoimmune disorder and regaining her eyesight to escaping an abusive marriage, Patricia experienced God's miraculous power. Her story is a testament to the life-changing impact of faith in Christ, and she hopes to inspire others to trust in Jesus for their own healing and restoration.

I grew up in Colombia, raised in a Catholic family without a Bible at home, where the name of God was professed without really knowing Him deeply. I have seen much superficial religiosity and empty life in the Catholic Church.

I started to have a genuine relationship with Jesus when I stopped all resistance and opened my heart. After I confessed each of my sins directly to Jesus and sincerely commenced loving Him, I could see His mighty power working in me. He began to bring healing in all areas of my life. Soon after I completely surrendered to Him, I came out of the prison I was living in.

Revelation 3:20, *"Here I am! I stand at the door and knock. If anyone hears my voice and opens the door, I will come in and eat with that person, and they with me"*, came true and alive for me in 2014. Jesus knocked at the door, wanting to have dinner with me, and I welcomed Him.

I had an autoimmune disease derived from Lupus, and I remember that I could not get out of bed one day. My dear sister Andrea prayed for me and spoke about Jesus Christ. I remember that the first miracle that the Lord did was to give me peace that surpasses all understanding. I believed in Him with all my strength, knowing I would rise above any situation. Soon after my sister prayed for me, the Lord healed my autoimmune disorder. All praise to God!

God performed great miracles in my life where I experienced healings, and I could see His power over me. Years later, I realised it happened as it is said in Acts 16:31, "Believe in the Lord Jesus, and you will be saved - you and your household". My sister turned to Jesus ten years earlier than me, and today my entire family believes in Jesus and was saved after seeing my life change for the better. I have become like a child who believes everything and knows that what comes from Father will be genuine and fulfilling.

Eyesight Restored

I have experienced many of God's miracles in my life that I am grateful for, but I would like to share how my eyesight was restored in 2016. This was the turning point when I realised that God is real. By profession, I am a civil engineer. My eyesight was damaged after being overexposed to the dust and sun most of the time. The epithelial membrane was torn, and no doctors could help me. Without any hope from the doctors, I turned to God for help.

I prayed and believed that the Lord would restore my eyesight. Then, one day, I felt the healing happening in my eyes. I knew this was happening because I felt as if someone had put stitches in my eyes. The next day I went to see my doctor, and I told him about my stitches experience. He examined my eyes, and he found that I had a scar which was in the process of healing, called cicatrisation.

As a result of this experience, my eyesight was completely restored. That was when I realised the King's power and understood that you could receive healing for yourself and others.

Rescued from an Abusive Marriage

I was married to an Italian man who had problems with excessive alcohol and drug abuse. We lived a stormy life. Though it was harsh and painful, I was able to forgive my ex-husband. In his alcohol and drug madness, he was always very abusive to me, and I suffered a lot in this toxic relationship.

One day, I could not stand it anymore, and I left. It was not easy for me, but God was there to raise me up. It was difficult because there was all the pain of the loss of companionship, but I knew new opportunities were coming. With God, every day is a new beginning. I had to move on.

God healed me of all the wrongs I could have done, and I no longer needed to take extreme measures to end my life. For the time I stayed in this toxic marriage, I harboured suicidal thoughts because I could not see any way out. But God empowered and freed me from the strong clutches.

Back on Track

I was in a trial period for many years until He made me demolish the fortresses that had imprisoned me. He broke off all the shackles and enabled me to live free with and through Jesus daily.

Now I am on the right track. I am happy, calm, and patient; I have found infinite peace. God also brought me the right man who loves me and loves Jesus. We are doing life and ministry together.

Today I can proclaim God's eternal life because I have seen it, I witnessed the power of God with my eyes and through my hands. I know that my Father wanted to make me testify of His miraculous works to encourage others to believe that Jesus can save and restore lives. I will never be silent in proclaiming that God is the King of Glory - The Creator and Jehovah with vast armies of angels.

As His committed disciple and an active part of the army of God, His Holy Spirit runs through my veins, stimulating every aspect of my being.

The love that He first gave me is ever alive so that His Gospel may be spread, preached, and proclaimed throughout the world in every language without ceasing.

God took me out of an abusive marriage, healed me, and gave me a new life. You can have your miracle too! Genuinely believe in Jesus and see what amazing things He will do for you.

We love because he first loved us.

1 John 4:19

Drawn to the Light: Finding Hope After Trauma

After growing up in an atheistic household and battling substance abuse, Steven experienced a profound dream that revealed Jesus to him, though he continued down a path of self-destruction. It wasn't until his wife encountered God and Steven sought the truth for himself that his life began to change. Through surrendering to Christ, Steven found forgiveness, healing, and purpose. His story is a testimony of the power of faith to bring hope and restoration, even after years of trauma and addiction.

When I was around five years old, my mum and dad divorced. To this day, I am not sure exactly why. Dad, at the time, was an assistant minister of a church in Wood Green, London. Mum remarried when I was around 7, and I grew up in more of an atheistic household. I was primarily interested in knowledge and philosophy, and I was dismissive of faith and the existence of God, mainly believing this could have caused my parents' marriage to break up.

When I reached 13, I smoked my first cannabis joint and started drinking when I was 14. As I reached my late teens, I was stoned on weed almost daily, using cocaine, pills, LSD, and often getting drunk. It was my way of escaping the world. It may have looked like I was happy, but inside I was lonely and had no real purpose, meaning, or direction in life. I was going from one job to another without being able to keep one.

One night, in my mid-20s, I had a dream. In the dream, I met this being - although I could not define His features, His face was radiant. Life and light itself were just flowing out of Him. As I woke that morning, I felt tears of joy and love; it was indescribable and overwhelming. I knew in my heart that this Being was Jesus.

Despite having this experience, I continued abusing drugs and did not want to stop.

At around 27, I met my girlfriend, Rachel, who is now my wife. She did not know much about my bad habits. One day she said, "I'd like to go to church". She was from a Catholic background but she was not born again. Shortly after this, a stranger approached me in the street and said, "You need to go to church". I replied, "No, I don't, but my partner does". So, I advised Rachel about this, and she ended up going with a friend.

Attracted by the Light

That night Rachel went to church, and, as usual, I was stoned, but as she returned, I noticed something had changed. She was radiant, glowing, and then I understood that she was filled with The Holy Spirit on that day. The darkness in me reacted, and I became jealous. I said, "You need to choose God or me". With little hesitation, Rachel looked at me and said, "There's no comparison". It was a big slap in the face to my pride and ego. I soon began to understand that I knew nothing about faith.

As time passed, I began seeking evidence of God's existence. My first recalled prayer was, "God, if You exist, please show Yourself to me". He did it in so many ways. One of the ways was through the Bible, which I read almost cover to cover. Although I did not fully understand its contents, it became clear that it was more real than anything I had ever studied.

On the 8th of February 2008, I decided to give my life entirely to Jesus. Privately I told God I would give Him my whole life. Publicly I repented and turned away from my old life and sin. At that moment, I experienced the Holy Spirit filling me and was overwhelmed with peace. It was like a dam broke that had been building up inside of me. I had broken every one of the ten commandments in my life. Nobody told me, but I knew in my heart that I was forgiven. I got baptised, and the old Steve had to die. Since that day, my life has been filled with joy, purpose and meaning. God has been transforming me, and many people from my past have said I have changed so much.

God has done many great things in my life: physical healing, miracles, and people set free from demons. I have witnessed thousands of people responding to the gospel and hundreds becoming born again. God is also using me to disciple others. He has shown me His love, and I can never go back. I have seen too much.

He died for all, that those who live should live no longer for themselves, but for Him who died for them and rose again.

2 Corinthians 5:15

Struggling with Faith: From Abuse to Redemption

Roy's story is one of profound redemption after years of anger, abuse, and disbelief. Deeply scarred by traumatic experiences in his childhood, including abuse at the hands of those he thought were religious, Roy was bitter and resentful towards Christianity. Despite his resistance, his wife prayed fervently for 17 years, asking God to reach Roy's heart. In 2014, Roy had a life-changing encounter with Jesus that shattered his misconceptions. Everything changed in that moment.

Whenever my wife urged me to turn to Jesus, I laughed, mocked, and ridiculed her stupidity. She could always expect a fight and tirade of abuse. Yet, she prayed for me almost every day. Most days, she was up at 5 am, on her knees, praying to Jesus, asking

Him to save me. I could not understand what she was talking about because I did not believe in Jesus.

Whenever my wife asked me to join anything to do with 'Christians', I refused most of the time, saying, "Christians are hypocrites, money makers, child abusers, molesters, rapists, and what part do I have with them?" Still, I was attending churches and doing religion.

I often retorted: "Why are these American mega-church pastors asking us to pay when they travel in luxury jets? Why did the Pope not do anything during World War II? Why did European people - who call themselves 'civilized' and myself 'uncivilised' as an Asian - send millions of Jews to the incinerator? Why are you trying to persuade me to be a 'Christian', as I am already a 'Christian'? Why can't people love each other rather than judge each other? If your God is real, why is there such anarchy, poverty, and indifference in the world today? What is the point of Jesus? What is the difference between Christians and any other religious group? They are all the same! Why are you talking about hell and trying to scare me? Why can't you just leave me alone?". These were the questions I was asking my wife when she was talking to me about Jesus and Christianity.

Raped and Abused

I had a pretty bad experience with the Roman Catholic Church. At the age of 7, I was gang-raped in the churchyard by so-called 'Christians' and went on to be molested and abused by Roman Catholic priests and other people for a few more years, and I hated it. At that time, I was asking where God was in all this. Religion had failed me entirely. All this time, I measured who God was, is, and is to be by the actions and behaviour of others. I never sought God for myself and never read the Bible to find God and what God is saying.

Answer to Prayer

My wife could not stop talking about Jesus, and I hated her for her insistence. For 17 years she prayed for me, waking up at 5 am most days, seeking God on her knees. God answered her prayers on the 20th of September 2014 at 11:30 am when Jesus spoke to me. The rest is history, as they say.

The God I met was nothing like I had heard about from other people. He is a loving God who wants to save us from sin and hell and wants to give us all a new life, eternal life. God proved to me many promises in the Bible, including visions and dreams, healings, and the power of His Word over Satanists, witch doctors, and freemasons who were rolling on the floor at the name of Jesus.

I experienced what was written in the Bible when I put my pride and arrogance aside by ditching the old Roy with all the titles, let go of my views, opinions, and experiences and started to seek God.

It was amazing. My mind could not get it when Jesus spoke to me in visions in broad daylight and through dreams, gave me a new language to communicate with Him, asked me to get baptised for the right reasons, and led me by His Spirit.

Many people have experienced healing at the mention of the name of Jesus, and many demons have been cast out from people in His name.

You can meet the same Jesus today!

Each time I mention hell, people say I bring fear, not love. But it is the love that will take the fear away, and the love of my wife Sangeeta and God stopped me from going to hell for eternity. It is a choice we have to make. Seek God for yourself.

God has done everything for you. Now it is your turn to receive Jesus; He is the way to Heaven. He has given you a free choice to go to Hell or to be with Him in Heaven forever. What matters most is that you will have to answer to God on the day of Judgement.

Why don't you take a step towards Jesus today? Find out if there is anything "good" about the Good News of Jesus. It is a choice everyone has to make. The choice is yours.

But small is the gate and narrow the road that leads to life, and only a few find it.

Matthew 7:14

CHAPTER 3 – ADDICTION & SUBSTANCE ABUSE

◉ Rescued from Alcohol, Depression, and Suicidal Thoughts
◉ From the Streets to Salvation: Escaping Drugs and Gangs
◉ From a Criminal Drug Addict to a Son of God
◉ From Rebellion and Theft to Divine Redemption

Even in the darkest valleys, God's light shines brightest. No matter how broken or lost you feel, His love can restore and renew. Trust in His plan, for He can turn every trial into a testimony, and every struggle into strength. With God, hope is never out of reach.

Rescued from Alcohol, Depression, and Suicidal Thoughts

Roz's story is one of deliverance from the depths of addiction, depression, and spiritual confusion. For years, she battled alcoholism and suicidal thoughts, seeking peace through alcohol, occult practices, and New Age spirituality. Despite trying every possible remedy, Roz remained empty and lost—until she turned to Jesus Christ. After a powerful encounter with God in 2018, Roz found the freedom, peace, and purpose she had been searching for.

I believe there are two types of depression, and I have experienced both in my life.

One is where the anguish, the hopelessness, and the darkness are all-consuming. You can see no way out. The pain of living is so intense, and you believe suicide is the only way out.

The other kind of depression is where there are no emotions involved. You feel dead. You feel absolutely nothing and want nothing from your life. Zombie-like. Empty inside. You experiment with everything to find peace. From a place of despair, you will do anything to feel something.

In the last ten years of my life as an alcoholic, from age 30 to 40, I was suicidal and did attempt suicide.

I experienced the second type of depression after my beloved mother died. Four years after her passing, I was empty inside. When I cried out to God to help me during both bouts of depression, He rescued me! He reached down to me on both occasions and pulled me out of the quicksand of my despair.

Let me tell you something - there is no shame in addiction. There is no shame in depression.

It is only when the Holy Spirit lives in you that you understand that you are in spiritual warfare. The veil of deception is removed from your eyes. God is real.

Satan is real. You are either in the dark with Satan or in the light with Jesus. It is one or the other.

Occultism, Alcohol, and Suicidal Thoughts

Here is my story.

I was raised Catholic, so I always believed in God, but not once was I told that to become part of God's family, to be saved, you must repent, have full immersion baptism, and receive the Holy Spirit.

By my twenties, I owned and used tarot cards and had occult books. I would read about astral travelling, aliens and the supernatural. I was a binge drinker as soon as I started drinking alcohol, and I could not stop once I started. When I lost my beloved dad, alcohol numbed the pain. It would be years later that I properly grieved the loss of my amazing dad.

By the age of 30, I was an alcoholic. I drank morning, noon and night while working full-time and pretending to be normal. For seven years, I took

Propranolol for my anxiety and went through bottles and bottles of Rescue Remedy.

My anxiety was constant, even on the medication. I was suicidal for about seven years. I even tried to commit suicide but was found by my mother and brought to the hospital.

I became sober at 40 through AA (Alcoholics Anonymous) and consistent hourly and daily prayer. After three months, my anxiety disappeared completely. Thank You, Jesus!!!

I had eight wonderful years sharing a flat with my mum. I travelled a lot and felt in control. But when my life seemed to go well, I pulled away from God and became addicted to Hatha yoga, Bikram yoga, and Kundalini yoga. There was always a lost, empty feeling inside me. I qualified as a yoga teacher but eventually lost all interest in yoga. By this time, I was a workaholic. I needed sleeping tablets to sleep (for five years), had numerous psychic readings and hypnosis sessions, read astrology, crystal, the Law of Attraction and Feng Shui books, and used Smudge Sticks to clean' my aura. I walked around with crystals in my pockets. I was still trying to 'fix' myself.

I lost my beloved mum before I was 50. Through grief and exhaustion, I locked myself away for two years. I had zero interest in the world. Absolutely zero interest.

I had been to three spiritualist churches and watched lots of so-called conspiracy theories during this time. They opened my eyes to what is going on in this world. What a shock. Then a Christian testimony popped up in my YouTube feed. I watched hours of these testimonies.

After two years in my room, it hit me... I needed to take part in life again. But I just could not find the enthusiasm. It was a massive struggle for me. I did not want to do anything or be with anyone. I spent two years looking for an anchor to get me back into the stream of life. Eventually, I started doing yoga again, practising shamanism (applying frog poison to burned skin, then vomiting violently), Chakra balancing, Mantra chanting and Qi Gong - I even intended to become a teacher.

I had been on an Ayahuasca retreat in Spain as well. I was taking Valium and magic mushrooms (micro-dosing), and I had become very promiscuous, dating and having sex with anyone I met.

No matter what I tried, nothing seemed to work. I felt depressed and empty. I was about to start micro-dosing on Acid tablets which were supposed to alleviate depression.

I was still watching Christian testimonies and wanted to know how people got God in their life. I had bought a Bible and gave up working on the Sabbath. Trying to find God, I went to a church service where they said you could receive the Holy Spirit, but nothing happened.

Then in 2018, I found out that all this New Age stuff I was doing was demonic; it all went against God. I heard that everything I was doing was causing my depression and lethargy. This news broke me. My 'crutches' were gone. How could I do life without these crutches?

At that moment, I knew for sure God was the Only Way. I broke down crying, begging God to come and get me. He did, but differently from the way I expected. Two hours later, the movie 'The Last Reformation - The Beginning' popped up in my YouTube feed. Watching this film, I realised two things: firstly, God was using those people, and secondly, I wanted God to use me. I contacted someone from the movie immediately and got baptised just three days later, on June 30th, 2018.

A New Life Doing What Jesus Did

My only crutch now is God, and I have never been happier. That emptiness, lethargy, and depression are no longer there. God has changed me entirely and supernaturally. I have peace and contentment now. God is real, and He is using me.

My life is now like The Last Reformation movie. But most importantly, I have a close relationship with God.

Call out to Jesus today. He will rescue you from your pain, phobias, addictions, disease, anxiety, depression, isolation, and confusion. You must cry out to Him and change your ways. Believe, trust and follow Jesus.

Be baptised as an adult and receive the Holy Spirit. Only then will you truly be set free and become a child of God. You will be able to have a personal relationship with God and get to spend eternity in Heaven with Him.

Doing good deeds will not get you to Heaven, but Jesus will. Jesus is the answer to everything that is wrong with you.

"Come to me, all you who are weary and burdened, and I will give you rest".

Mathew 11:28

From the Streets to Salvation: Escaping Drugs and Gangs

Raised in a Christian home but disillusioned by the hypocrisy he witnessed and the boredom he felt, Jamie sought adventure and escape through destructive paths. He became a "tough" kid, hiding his true self, losing his identity in drugs, gangs, and anger. Yet, even at his lowest, God had a plan for him. Through the love and guidance of new friendships and a renewed faith, Jamie's life was turned around. Today, his story serves as a reminder of the transformative power of God's grace and the strength that comes from finding salvation in Christ.

I was brought up as a Christian. My parents attended a big church in Bracknell, but I disliked church for multiple reasons:

- I found it very boring.

- I could not relate to it as a young man. The activities felt slightly too middle-class and proper. I wanted adventure and wildness.

- My mum and dad did not have a good relationship. I saw them as hypocrites, praising God in the morning and arguing in the afternoon.

My mum and dad's relationship affected me as a young man. I was also very insecure, sensitive, bookish, and impressionable.

Trying to Fit In

I was bullied at secondary school and struggled to fit in. I then decided to become one of the "tough" kids. I hid myself, losing my identity for about five years. I hid my love for books and rebelled at school. I spent most of my school years outside the classroom or playing truant. I was often high on drugs in school, and I continued to become angrier and angrier. I continued drinking, taking drugs, stealing, and getting into fights.

I left school with minimal qualifications, despite having a sharp mind. My mum and dad got divorced soon after I finished school. It was a massive relief but also tricky for my brothers and me. At the same time, I felt guilty because I thought, rightly or wrongly, that it was my fault due to my behaviour.

I began the process of change slowly. I managed to go to university and became more confident. However, during my first year, I felt incredibly lonely at university. I began to get severely depressed and felt an emptiness in my soul.

I contemplated taking my own life.

God Had a Plan

That year I was back from university for New Year's Eve. I had nowhere to go as I had severed contact with many of my school friends. My mum's friend Janine, who was a genuine and faith-filled Christian, realised that I was at home alone and asked her daughter to invite me to her party.

The party was unremarkable (having no alcohol or likely hook-ups), but I met two incredibly special people that night. Their names were Liam and Rory. I saw instantly that there was something different about them. I realised they were Christians, and then I started to contemplate the Christian faith, despite my previous misgivings.

I began to attend church every Sunday with my mum and little brother. A few weeks in, I gave my life to Christ, and my life changed forever. I was discipled by Rory for many years, served in his church, and went on mission trips with him.

Eventually, I went to the Kerith Community Church to do a Bible Course, where I met my wife, Marija.

We then served the church for four years and were part of a team that planted a church in Egham/Hythe, where we continue to serve there today.

Therefore, if anyone is in Christ, the new creation has come: The old has gone, the new is here!

2 Corinthians 5:17

From a Criminal Drug Addict to a Son of God

This is the powerful testimony of a man called James, who once lived a life consumed by crime, addiction, and despair. Raised in a dysfunctional environment, he sought identity in gangs and the streets, falling deeper into a world of drugs, violence, and lawlessness. Despite reaching a point of extreme physical and emotional brokenness, he encountered the transformative love of Jesus Christ. His life was radically changed, and he now shares his story to inspire others, showing that no matter how lost one may feel, there is hope and redemption in Christ.

Introduction to a Life of Crime

I haven't always lived the life I live today. I was very much a man who never had any awareness of who God is or even that He existed—a man who wore many masks, whether that be as a master of pride, a very weak man who refused to show any weakness on the surface, a man who understood that violence was a way to deal with situations, a man bound by all kinds of different drugs, bound to the criminal lifestyle, and bound to being a menace in society. I was a man who looked and reached for all different avenues as ways to step away from the life I lived. Nothing worked for me, but what did work was Jesus Christ. And this is my testimony.

My testimony is me testifying of what the Lord Jesus Christ has done for me.

I've not always been an evangelist; I've not always been a Christian—definitely not. I grew up in a household that was very dysfunctional. I grew up with a lot of alcoholism around me. I grew up very troubled by a lot of abuse—physical, mental, and emotional. From a very young age, in school, I was a very troubled child, very disruptive, and caused many problems, being excluded from many schools in the past.

I grew up from the age of 15 selling drugs, and at 16, I moved out of my household and moved in with local drug dealers, where I felt like I found identity in gangs and on the streets. The streets were where I was most of the time, whether that be selling drugs, getting into petty crimes at the beginning, or chilling with people on the streets, and that's where I felt like I found my identity. After a short amount of time, one of my friends told me about these raves that used to happen in warehouses. They told me about these raves that were illegal, where you could take drugs, and no one would stop you, and you were free to do whatever you wanted.

I spent a lot of time in these places, meeting the people there, and eventually, I got to a place where I was organizing these raves.

Descent into Drug Addiction

The more I grew in the criminal world, the more the drugs increased. I started off with MDMA, then went on to cocaine, and before I knew it, I got my life into a position where I was taking crack and heroin. I remember a time when I was sitting on the streets begging, and a man came up to me and spoke to me about taking a job—that job was selling drugs in nightclubs. The security allowed us to do it.

As I was being paid, I progressed in that area of life, in that criminal way of living, to the point that I was selling drugs in multiple nightclubs. I had people selling drugs for me. I was buying firearms just in case anything happened, getting into fights in nightclubs. My ego and pride were growing and growing to the point where if there was another dealer in the nightclub, I would begin a fight with them and get the security to kick them out.

Life got really, really bad for me. It got to the point where I was about 45 kilos—I was very skinny. I remember I went to see my dad in Devon after a very long time. I stayed in a hotel there because I didn't want to stay at my dad's house; I wanted to continue being able to drink alcohol and take drugs without anyone telling me I couldn't.

I met my dad for breakfast once, and when I met him, he didn't know what had happened to me—he didn't understand why I was so skinny. He was very disappointed, but I was under a lot of delusion at the time. I was in a position in life where I didn't even see what other people saw.

When I looked in the mirror, I didn't see that there was an issue. I was filled with so much pride and ego that I didn't think anything was wrong with me.

The Turning Point: Kidnapping and Recovery

It got so bad that the drugs began to run out, and I didn't even have money to sell drugs anymore, so I had to start robbing people for drugs. That brought in a different ballgame; there was a lot of violence—it got to the point where I ended up getting kidnapped. When I got kidnapped, I was beaten for the course of four hour, having all kinds of weapons used against me—I got stabbed twice in my leg and lower leg. Things got really bad, but during that time I felt an essence of peace; I felt like everything was going to be okay.

When I left there, I ran to my friend's house and collapsed at his door. My face was completely disfigured, I was running down with blood, and I got into resuscitation and was throwing up blood. I remember my mum looking at me, wondering what was wrong, and if I was going to be okay. The doctors were looking at her, knowing that throwing up blood in resuscitation is not a good sign. However, after a couple of days, I ended up getting better and eventually came out of the hospital. COVID was in the hospital at that time, but I was so lost in the drug world that I didn't even know what was going on in the world. When I came out of the hospital, I was still taking drugs... I remember screaming and shouting on the streets, calling my family, trying to get money from them for drugs, until it came to the point where I got down on my knees and screamed out for help. I remember it like it was yesterday—I felt an overwhelming sensation of His presence, curled up into a foetus on the floor, crying and being comforted. From the moment I woke up the next day, I never used drugs again. The desire for drugs left me, and something new was happening inside me.

Today, I live a life where I go around telling people about this hope that I found in God. I'm here to encourage you right now: if God can save a wretched soul like me, He can do it for anyone. I knew about God long before I was in my bedroom and gave my life to Jesus Christ. For about 10 years, evangelists were coming my way—little messages were coming forth, and the Lord was drawing me to Him for a very long time; seeds were being sown over 10 years. Trust the Lord that no matter who you are, it doesn't matter what you've done—there is justification at the cross. Jesus says, "I paid the debt and wiped you clean." When you come to Him, He recreates you into a new creation. Life will never be the same.

"Therefore, if anyone is in Christ, he is a new creation; old things have passed away; behold, all things have become new."

2 Corinthians 5:17

Today, James White is an ordained CfaN Associate Evangelist. You can connect with him through Facebook.

From Rebellion and Theft to Divine Redemption

From a young age, John was raised by a devout mother who was a dedicated prayer warrior. Despite his early involvement in church activities, he struggled with a growing disconnect, fuelled by teachings that portrayed God as punishing. As a teenager, he led a double life—conforming to church expectations while falling into increasingly destructive behaviour with the wrong crowd. His life spiralled into crime, arrests, and a deepening sense of fear and shame. Yet, even as he drifted away from his faith, the persistent prayers of his mother and subtle, divine interventions began to work in his life, setting the stage for a remarkable transformation.

Early Life and Struggles with Faith

I remember attending church from about 6 years old. I was going to church, so I knew about Jesus from an early age. My mum was a prayer warrior. They were quite strict and religious. As I started to get older, I started to think differently but still went to church. I used to play the drums in church and enjoyed this. After a while, this wasn't enough to keep me there. Religion didn't appeal to me anymore. I used to hear teachings that God is punishing, and I was afraid of God.

In school, I began mixing with the wrong crowd and living a double life—one person with my friends and another in church. When I was around 12 or 13, I started getting into trouble, stealing chocolates from the local shop and selling them at school. My behaviour escalated as I continued mixing with the wrong people, leading to several arrests. I felt ashamed and embarrassed, and despite still attending church, I told myself I'd stop at 15—and I did. Although I was afraid of God, I continued stealing but also prayed the Lord's Prayer every night, something my mum taught me.

I thought my school friends were my real friends, not the church youth. Things quickly spiralled out of control as I started breaking into houses, selling stolen goods, and getting more deeply involved in crime. I was hiding the stolen jewellery underneath my wardrobe and spending the money in arcades. I didn't spend money on clothes because I didn't want my mom to see this.

Arrests and Legal Troubles

I was introduced to cannabis and started smoking regularly, which brought more police attention. They came to my house and found the money and the jewellery that I stole, so I got arrested. Things got really bad. I was going to juvenile court and my mum had to bail me out many times. I was so ashamed and embarrassed. Most of the times I was arrested in London, and there was a time I was arrested in Uxbridge early in the morning at 2am.

My mum was devastated, and despite her prayers and attempts to help, I couldn't stop myself. I now realise I was under demonic oppression, stealing not just for money but out of compulsion.

I had so many court cases… there were eight at some point in different juvenile courts.

From the moment I left church things got much worse. I had numerous court cases, and at 15, I was sent to a detention centre known as Short, Sharp, Shock. It was a place where I was abused and beaten without any reason. I was there for six weeks and after six week I went to court again for other cases when the judge said he was considering sending me back to this place. He put me in the cell until he came to a decision. I remember right there in my cell, I went to God and I said to Him, "If you deliver me from not being sent back to that juvenile prison, I will give my life to you and become a Christian". Then I went back in front of the judge who said he was really considering sending me back, but he changed his mind and gave me another chance; he set me free. As I was going out with my mother, God reminded me of what I promised - that I will give my life to Him. I said something that even now it makes me shudder... I said, "Yes, Lord, I did say that, but I didn't say when I will do that". I suppose I thought I could outsmart God... I didn't hear anything else from God after that, but He bore with me and found a different way years later to draw me back.

I continued my destructive lifestyle, stealing and getting into more trouble. Then there was a time when a friend of mine persuaded me to buy an air gun, which I was taking to school even though I wasn't allowed. I was even robbing people at school to give me money. One day, I was shooting birds, and the neighbours saw me at the window. I hid the gun in my wardrobe and my mum found it and broke it into pieces.

Soon after that, I did some reflections and realised I was getting arrested only when I was with other people, so I started stealing on my own. This carried on all throughout my teenage years.

I used to hang around on the streets, and my mum was trying to keep me in, but I always managed to trick my mum to get out. I continued committing offenses, giving my mum a lot of problems.

Continued Rebellion and Consequences

I was well hooked into cannabis; I was smoking weed every single day in the morning and after each meal. I was stealing to buy drugs, and I was going out a lot. I didn't like being at home, I liked being out on the streets going to parties. There was a time when someone showed me a knife which is now banned in the UK. It was knife that opened and closed quickly. This man was showing me lots of tricks and moves, and I was amazed by what he did. After a while, I bought one myself and practiced how to use it. I kept practising every night until I got better than him. I thank God I didn't have to use it. Whenever I entered any fights, I didn't have the knife with me.

There were many times in my life when I called out to God to help me, and He did. He helped me.

I lived a life when I loved being a thief and doing what I was doing, I loved the status and the respect on the streets. Everything I was doing was evil. I was around violent people, so I witnessed violent acts.

My life was getting out of hand, but I had a praying mother. She never gave up on me. I do believe if my mum wouldn't have been how she was, I wouldn't have made it. That's way I know prayer is powerful - prayer works.

There was a time when I went out for a rave and went into the house quietly not to wake up anyone. I got home at 2am and heard my mum praying; I heard her praying for me. She asked God to save me, to protect me, to turn my life around. This didn't change me. I went back into my room and continued with my life.

I remember one time when I went to my friends' house everyone was taking different type of drugs. I was 18 years old. That was the time when I said to myself, "it must be more to life than this". Then I heard, "Yes, there is. Try Jesus". I remembered what I knew about Jesus when I was in church, but I remember it was boring - I didn't like this, so I didn't pursue this thought.

I had many God moments. One time, when I was 20, I came back home after I stole things, and my mum was in the kitchen worshipping. It was for the first time when, all of a sudden, I realised that what I was doing was wrong. The Holy Spirit was present. I went to my room, convicted by the Holy Spirit, thinking that it was wrong what I am doing and was wondering how bad the person I stole things from must feel when he realises these things were missing. Soon after, the devil came and spoke to me saying, "What's the matter with you? Why are you thinking like this? You are a thief. You've got money, enjoy what you have". I believed what I heard and continued with my bad life. God was calling me at that time, but I didn't know what to do. I went out and continued living my life bad.

A Turning Point

A big change in my life came when I turned 21. I had a few stolen goods in my house and one evening I met with a friend who said he can sell some of the things I had. So he dropped by my home to pick up the goods. I took some of the stuff and walked towards his car. What I didn't realise was that police were following him. I showed him the things in the car, and a few minutes later the car was surrounded by the police, who asked us to come out. The police found the stuff in the car, and I said they were mine. There was no room to escape. They arrested me and took me to the station. They took me to my house to check for other goods. The sadness in my mum's eyes broke my heart. They went into my room and found all the other stolen things, including a knife and products that have been banned in the UK. I was taken to the police station and then to court. After that, I was taken to the adult prison. Until then, I was only in juvenile prison, which was different. That period was dreadful. I realised I was in big trouble, and I asked God to help me. He did intervene, but I didn't change immediately.

I was spending all day in the cell. One time, after I moved from prison to the police station in Middlesbrough because the prison got too full, a friend and I went on a hunger strike until they were looking to give us better conditions. After 3 and a half days, they let us come out and go to the courtyard and allowed us to watch television on the weekend.

I was in and out of prison at Wormwood Scrubs and Brixton HMP. When I came out of the prison last time, I moved into my own flat. I still did wrong things but a bit less risky.

In the next few years, God started to call me—things started to happen. Christians were coming to me and telling me about Jesus. I managed to escape all the time. At home, I was pondering why there were so many Christians trying to talk to me.

One woman I liked persistently shared her faith with me, eventually bringing me back to the very church I had left as a child. I started attending church and playing drums but was hesitant to fully commit to God.

Final Surrender and Redemption

I was going to church but didn't like the altar calls. For about a year and a half, I was afraid to give my life to the Lord, even though there were so many times when I felt I should give my life to Jesus.

However, I made a commitment that if God brought me to a new year, I would give my life to Him. Don't try to do this—give your life to Jesus now.

During that time between my commitment and when I gave my life to Jesus, the devil tried to take my life many times… There were accidents happening, but the angels pushed me and saved me. There were so many accidents happening to me that even my managers noticed. Things were falling down, and if they would've hit me, I would have died, but supernaturally they were pushed to the side to make sure I was not harmed and could fulfil my promise.

Then the time came, and I gave my life to Jesus. The Lord helped me change my character; He continues to change me. I was fearless in stealing, but when I came to the Lord, I was fearful of evangelizing, of telling others about Jesus, but He moulded me and shaped me to be bold.

"He also brought me up out of a horrible pit, out of the miry clay, and set my feet upon a rock, and established my steps. He has put a new song in my mouth—Praise to our God; many will see it and fear, and will trust in the Lord."

Psalm 40:2-3

CHAPTER 4 – SUPERNATURAL ENCOUNTERS WITH GOD

- From Sikhism to Salvation: A Journey of Faith and Divine Encounters
- From Islam to Jesus. Powerful Encounters with The Lord
- From Doubting God to Moving in Power and Making Disciples of Christ

Supernatural encounters with God are moments when heaven touches earth, revealing His power and presence in ways beyond human understanding. In these divine moments, doubts are shattered, hearts are transformed, and we are reminded that God is not distant—He is actively moving, speaking, and inviting us to experience the extraordinary in the midst of the ordinary.

From Sikhism to Salvation: A Journey of Faith and Divine Encounters

Raised in a non-Christian household, Rajvir encountered God after watching videos about Satanism in the music industry. Curiosity led him to pray to Jesus, and he immediately felt peace. Though initially identifying as Sikh, Rajvir found that when he prayed to Jesus, his prayers were answered. A pivotal moment came when Rajvir prayed for his brother, who had a vision of heaven, confirming Christian truths. This strengthened Rajvir's faith, eventually leading his entire family to embrace Christianity. His story highlights God's miraculous power and the profound changes that faith in Jesus brought to his life.

Visit to Heaven

The Lord has been good to me in all the kindness he has shown me. Born in 1998, I was raised in a Non-Christian household - Dad, Mum, my younger brother, and I. Growing up, if anybody had asked me what religion I was, I would have said I was a Sikh. I would occasionally go to the temple, do a couple of religious events in the year, and wear the metal 'Kara' on my arm. I believed God existed, but I had no personal relationship with him.

I developed a routine of reciting a prayer to 'God' most nights before I went to bed, but I did not know what I was saying because it was in Punjabi.

That all changed in 2013.

Satanism in the Music Industry

I was 14 at the time; it was the summer holidays. I was staying at my grandmother's house, watching videos on YouTube. One day a video came up in my feed about Satanism in the Music Industry. After watching the video, I started watching more and more about this topic. It was interesting and not something we think much about. Some of the music we love to listen to has some of the strangest video content, and we cannot understand why. The videos I watched were made by Christians who explained the Satanic elements in the music.

These videos would usually end with a prayer someone could pray to accept Jesus into their life, at which point I would often move on to the next video. Eventually, after watching so many videos over a few days, I realised how strongly Satanism was promoted in these music videos. It was not a 'one-off' feature. I was scared.

What if it is all real? What if Heaven and Hell are real? There must have been a reason why these music videos were promoting Satan, and why do they go against Jesus? Why not oppose other religious faiths?

Jesus - Better than the Evil One

Being scared, I decided to find the prayer to accept Jesus into my heart. I went to my room and whispered this prayer so nobody else would hear me. My head cleared up as soon as I finished praying, and I was at peace. Fear was gone. I had never had this happen to me before. Now I was at a crossroads because I had identified myself as a Sikh all my life. I was not looking to abandon my Sikh faith, but I could not deny what I had just experienced after praying to Jesus.

I resorted to a test: I would pray to the Sikh God, then pray to the Christian God. I found nothing happened when I prayed to the Sikh God. I was closing my eyes and talking to the ceiling. But when I prayed to the Christian God, the Heavenly Father, it was a completely different experience. My prayers were answered; something was happening; my Spirit was alive. It was unlike anything I had ever known in my life. God was real; he was listening to my prayers and answering them. He was my Heavenly Father, I was one of his children, and I was safe. I was a secret believer in Jesus in my house for about one and a half years. My immediate family did not know about my faith in Jesus.

At that time, the Lord was so patient and kind to me. He answered my prayers, and the Holy Spirit was with me; it was incredible.

Brother saw Heaven

Towards the end of 2014, I started thinking that I should share my faith with my parents. The problem I faced was fear. I had thoughts on how I would break the news to my dad, but God had other plans.

It was soon after New Year; I was still on my Christmas half-term break. My brother and I were in our room, awake one night. I asked him if I could pray for him, and he allowed me to. He was lying in bed and closed his eyes. I put my hand on him and started praying, but I was praying in my mind.

As I was praying, I told Jesus that my brother would believe things if he saw them, so I asked the Lord Jesus to show my brother Heaven. A few moments later, I tried to speak to my brother, and he responded, "Bro, don't disturb me; I'm seeing Heaven". My heart filled with joy hearing this, and I was crying. It had not even been ten minutes, and Jesus answered my prayer. It was incredible. My brother started describing what he saw in Heaven. Eventually, he told me that he could see God.

He could not see God's face, but he described God as light, which is what we find in the Bible (Exodus 33:20 and 1 John 1:5). After that, he told me that he saw Jesus. He did not speak to Jesus verbally, but it was telepathic.

Now my brother was not a Christian, he did not know who I was praying to or what I was praying for, and he did not know what the Bible said about God, yet here he was stating specifically Christian details.

After going to Heaven, my brother started crying, saying he had felt like he was the most special person in all the world. He was only ten years old at the time.

Within the next few nights, I asked him if he wanted to go to Heaven again. On that second night, my brother went to Heaven again. After going to Heaven a second time, my brother wanted to pray for me to go to Heaven. I accepted his offer; he put his hand on me and prayed for me. But nothing happened. It turns out he had prayed to the Sikh God, which is why nothing happened.

After persuading him to pray to Jesus, he prayed for me, and I felt very different inside. I felt like I was falling. I felt so scared that I stopped my brother from praying. From then on, I went through a difficult time when I felt like I was going to die. I was terrified. I had struggled to sleep and was incredibly fearful.

During this time, I shared my belief in Jesus with my parents. Because of their worry for me at the time, they did not respond as strongly as they could have. My faith was not a priority for them at the time.

After nearly a month of struggling, I went to my room and prayed to God the Father about this issue. I prayed that if this was to do with my brother praying for me to go to Heaven, I did not want to go to Heaven until the day I died, so when I enter, I never have to leave again. From that night on, there was a significant change, and I had such a peaceful night of sleep.

After that period of trouble, a new issue surfaced in the house. My parents wanted me to return to being a Sikh, but I was not prepared to return.

I had seen Jesus do too much. Going back to my old religion was not right for me. This conflict of interest was not without its arguing, anger, and disagreements. The difference in faith lasted for much of 2015.

It was not until the end of 2015 that my dad accepted Jesus into his life, and my mum believed in

Jesus soon after. Since then, we have seen and heard the Lord doing miracles in our lives and those around us.

After coming to Jesus, my life changed. I walk into situations with God by my side. God encourages me and answers my prayers; it is real life with Him. There is so much I could share about how good Jesus has been to me and how much He did. I know God changed me for the better from where I was all those years ago. That is something God does; He changes us from the inside out. We are 'sanctified', and, in the process, God cleans us and makes us better people. He fills us with His Holy Spirit and 'sanctifies' us by His Holy Spirit. God has been so gracious to us as a family, he has been so kind and loving.

Now, this is eternal life: that they know you, the only true God, and Jesus Christ, whom you have sent.

John 17:3

From Islam to Jesus. Powerful Encounters with The Lord

Jahir dedicated his life to memorizing the Quran and living as a faithful Muslim. However, after spending time with his Christian friend and attending church out of respect, Jahir began to experience a deep spiritual awakening. Despite his initial resistance, a powerful dream of Jesus and miraculous healing encounters changed his life. Through these supernatural experiences, Jahir came to believe in Jesus as his Saviour, leaving behind his Muslim faith despite the consequences. Today, Jahir is a dedicated follower of Christ, sharing the gospel and leading others to Jesus.

My name used to be Jahir Islam, but God told me to change my surname to Israel, so I did what He said. I was a devout Muslim throughout my life. Every day from age 5, I went to the mosque to learn Arabic and Quranic recitation. I also attended an Islamic school of Quranic memorisation – I was training to be Hafiz (One who has memorised the Quran). I memorised about half of the Quran from 12 to 15. It was always my dream to go to Heaven and work my way up to be the most faithful Muslim I could be.

I kept away from all forms of evil, including smoking, drinking, women, and so forth, and I would always pray extra in addition to the five daily prayers. My parents noticed my strong desire to be an Islamic Scholar and Hafiz and felt quite concerned and uncomfortable as my focus swayed away from my education (specifically GCSEs). Because of this, they decided to end my Islamic career.

From that point, I was quite depressed but swiftly shifted my focus to school, career, and ambition to perform well academically. Then I studied

Mathematics at the degree level for four years at a university in London.

At the university, I longed to make good Muslim friends; unfortunately, all Muslims I associated with were lukewarm. All were frustrated to see how strong and disciplined in Islamic teaching I was and would bully and mock me. So, I left that group of friends.

Soon after that, I started to associate with non-Muslims and hang around with them till the end of year 2. They also made fun of Islam. It was a nightmare.

For a few months, I had a YouTube channel to teach others how to become a good Muslim, highlighting the importance of taking religion seriously. My family thought I was too extreme. Everyone in Wales was gossiping about me, so without having any support, I got discouraged and stopped doing it. After that, I joined the Islamic society at university and pushed myself to get involved with them and be part of their prayers, talks, and lectures. My new Muslim friends were worldly and completely neglected every form of Islamic advice I would give to help them.

My Christian Friend

I got my first job at a call centre, where I stayed for ten months at least. My manager was great. At the time, he was a very worldly, intellectual and scientific person, coming from a Hindu background but atheistic in his belief. He left the company, and out of nowhere, I bumped into him months later, talked to him, and built a relationship with him.

I was concerned, furious, and sad when he told me he was now a Christian. As we became friends, we would visit each other and talk about our life and also religion. I tried hard to prove to him Tawhid (the belief in the oneness and unity of Allah as expressed in the first of the Five Pillars of Islam) via Quranic scriptures and why it is the truth, and he kept mentioning about his relationship with Jesus and the Gospel. I could not convince him, but deep inside, I was convicted and drawn to what he had. My heart was crying out for God in a relational way, so in prayer, I told Allah that I wanted to know him relationally and hear him. I decided to stop praying until I found out who God was, and as I tried to seek Him, I told Him that He could not punish me.

My friend invited me to several churches, and I went out of respect. Then I realised I was wrong in my fixated view of Christianity (which was Catholicism). I saw people falling, manifesting, healing, and worshipping from their hearts. I thought this was a cult, and it was demonic. He invited me again to church, and I went for him, but this time I felt something in my heart – it was very peaceful. I had a good experience but could not reveal it because of my pride. This church held a group at my university to meet Christians and talk. I went along and joined in with the worship but neglected the name Jesus when singing. However, while there, once again, I felt something in my heart.

Later, I had so much pain in my tooth, and as I told them, they immediately started laying hands on me and commanding healing, and I was healed. I was astonished but was still thinking this was demonic!

My Christian friend kept calling me about going to church, and I was so frustrated by his insistence and blocked him from reaching out to me for months. One day I suddenly bumped into him again in early 2017, and while he was on the phone, he told his sister that I was on his prayer list and that he was praying for me daily. Since then, we have become close friends.

My Secret Girlfriend

During that time, in 2015, I met my first girlfriend, a Polish girl at university. Being a Muslim, I was against this initially, but as I became more liberal and open to non-Muslims and various cultures, I started having deep conversations with her and fell in love. I entered a relationship which lasted for over three years. I tried converting her to Islam and wanted to marry her, but it did not work. I did everything in my strength and realised my words had no power because she was far from considering Islam. She was from a Catholic background but was very spiritual and into the New Age religion and was trying to convince me to have the same beliefs. I was curious.

During our relationship, I would visit my parents often but hide my relationship from them. I did this the whole time I was in a relationship with her. I knew there would have been severe consequences if they ever found out.

Fast-forward to three years after graduating and getting a job. I decided to visit and catch up with my family during a weekend in December 2017 – I never thought that weekend would be the change and transformation of my life!

The Truth Will Set You Free

I visited my parents the weekend of 9th - 10th of December 2017. My girlfriend called me at some point, so my mum became suspicious. I faltered and went to my room. While talking on the phone, I heard a movement underneath my door and suspected my mum was listening. So, I started to pretend that I was talking to a guy friend, but near the end of our conversation, I could not resist but say, "I love you", and ended the call. Smash! My mum opened the door and cried, "Do you have a girlfriend? Who is this girl?"

I lied and just said, "it's not a girl, just a guy friend", but she refused to believe me and kept asking.

I lied once more and said, "Okay, it is a girl, but just a friend talking about a project". Then, my mum said, "Please Jahir, tell me. We will not do anything bad. Don't lie! We're open to hearing what you have to say".

Never in my life have I heard the voice of God, but at that moment, I was silent, and suddenly I heard an authoritative, powerful voice in my ear saying, "TELL THE TRUTH".

I was confused and thought I was insane, but I knew it was a good thing, so I spat out the truth and said, "Yes, mum, I have a girlfriend. I love her, and I want to marry her. Please give her a chance. She will come to Islam gradually!"

I pleaded with my mum not to call my dad as he was aggressive and short-tempered, but she called him. I wanted to avoid any trouble, so I told my mum to leave and locked my door.

I could hear him verbally abusing my mum, swearing, yelling across the rooftops, and accusing her. As time passed, my parents consulted all family members about this and then called an imam to perform an exorcism on me and check if anything was wrong with me. They found nothing. In the morning, my younger sister called me to go downstairs as my dad requested.

Being hot-tempered, he gave me an ultimatum straight away. He said, "Jahir, you have two choices: leave the girl, your job and university, and come under this roof or leave us. If you do this, you will no longer be our son; we cut you off from our bloodline from this day on, and no one will tell you if we die. You have to decide within two to three hours; if not, I will force you out of the house".

I tried negotiating, but he would not accept this, so I just cried and rushed upstairs for help by calling my best Muslim friends, but none were willing to support or help but instead just said, "It's your life; you're an adult, we have problems, sorry". I understood but panicked and relied on my one Christian friend, previously my work manager. I knew he was passionate about God, loving and friendly, so I told him about my situation. Straight away, he started telling me about Jesus. He said that Jesus loves me, He died on the cross for me, and He wants a relationship with me.

My friend said that Jesus is real and He can save me. I was fuming because I had had enough of listening to this, so I muted the phone and screamed: "Jesus isn't the son of God. He's just a prophet!"

Feeling guilty for what I did, I unmuted him, and he said to me the words that pierced my heart: "Jahir, whether you believe it or not, it's the TRUTH! Do you want to know who God is and have a relationship with Him?"

I said, "Yes", and he said, "You have to cry out and ask Him with all your heart, and He will reveal Himself to you". I replied, "You're right; I have nothing to lose. It's not going to cost me anything. I want to know God", so we ended the call there.

I went down on my knees and cried out with all my heart and uttered, "Allah, I don't believe in you anymore, but GOD, I know you are real, just like my friend. JESUS, if you are the Way, the Truth and the Life, show me right now, show me in a dream that You are my LORD and Saviour and my GOD, and only then will I accept you, otherwise forget it!"

Then I challenged God and said, "GOD I'm going to go to bed now (it was only about 11:30 am), and I want to see You".

Supernatural Encounters with Jesus

So I did, and I immediately fell into a deep sleep. I saw myself in a dark place, with only Muslims in an airport (in a Muslim country perhaps) and out of nowhere, a Muslim gang of boys chased me with weapons and eventually pushed me down and beat me. I became paralysed, could not even scream while people were walking past me without care, and could only whisper, "Someone, help me".

A sudden bright light shone through the night sky and hit me - I was instantly healed. I looked up and saw a large human body figure dressed in a long white garment with long brown hair; from the face, all I could see was a powerful blinding light. I was scared and started to doubt, "This can't be Jesus; this isn't Jesus". As a Muslim, I had never read the Bible before, but I heard these words, He spoke:

"Your family will forsake you, but I never will; I am Jesus Christ your Father, and you are my son. I shed my blood for you all. Everyone knows about me, but they don't know who I am. Believe in me, and I will be with you forever. That's how much I love you, Jahir!"

I woke up and felt so much peace; however, I started to rub my eyes to clear them, and all I could see was darkness, although it was afternoon. I realised at that point that I had lost my sight. I was completely blind. I was panicking, crying, and screaming, but no one could hear me. Out of nowhere, I heard the voice of God audibly, and a light shone into my eyes - I was healed, and my vision was restored! Hallelujah JESUS.

After all of that, I still did not believe in Jesus and had too much fear of leaving Islam, thinking I would go to hell. That day was a Sunday. My uncle came later and tried convincing me to stay and not move, but I decided to stay with my girlfriend. They asked me to leave the family home if I made that decision, so I left my parents' house.

While on the couch, my Christian friend called me and told me to go to Golders Green station and join him at a house church where he was. He told me to let him know once I arrived at the station. When I arrived at the station, I realised my battery was dead. No one was willing to help me, and with no charge, I asked God, in my heart, to make a way, and amazingly my phone was restored with a call from my friend. He called a taxi for me, and then it died again, but it was what I needed to get to the house church.

Once I reached the house, I felt a sense of immense peace. I explained my story, and they were supportive, emotional, and affectionate. I was amazed. They advised me and then asked me if they could pray for me. I was gaining strength and peace, and finally, they asked me, "Do you want to accept Jesus Christ as your Lord and Saviour and repent from all your sins?"

I paused for a while, so fearful, but suddenly what was holding me back broke, and I accepted Jesus into my heart and repented. Peace just flowed through my body when I did this.

Demons Left and a New Life Began

A week or two later, I came again, and while everyone was praying, I heard tongues, which I thought was very weird. I was scared.

While others left, someone asked me if I wanted to speak in tongues and receive the Holy Spirit. I was hesitant at first but then accepted. They prayed and my leg started to shake aggressively as if a demon was leaving me (it was uncontrollable). It became increasingly intense, and I began to praise God as the

Holy Spirit entered me and flowed from my belly upwards out of my mouth, and I spoke in tongues.

I was baptized two weeks later, and I became a new creation. A photo of my baptism showed the light of God shining from my face as I arose from the water. I knew, confidently, that the God I serve now is the true living God.

Thank you, Jesus. Hallelujah to the Kings of Kings.

Today, Jahir is following Jesus and making disciples as he shares the gospel, heals the sick and teaches new believers what he knows.

Keep your lives free from the love of money and be content with what you have, because God has said,

> *"Never will I leave you;*
> *never will I forsake you."*

Hebrews 13:5

From Doubting God to Moving in Power and Making Disciples of Christ

A powerful story of transformation from doubt and sin to a life filled with the power of God. Despite growing up in the church and serving in leadership roles, Alexandru never had a personal relationship with God and lived a life of hypocrisy, mixing worship with sinful habits. Frustrated and disillusioned, he challenged God to prove His existence within a week—and God answered.

After a life-changing encounter with the Holy Spirit, Alexandru's faith was revived. He now leads a ministry where he regularly heals the sick and shares the gospel, living out his faith boldly. His story is a testament to God's grace and the life-altering impact of encountering His presence.

I grew up in the church from the age of nine and got increasingly involved over the years. I was a leader in the children's program, then a leader in the youth program, and, as I became an adult, a worship leader. I finished two Bible schools over four years and led several house church Bible studies.

Even though I was in church all that time and studied the Word of God, I must say that I had no personal relationship with God. I lived in sin.

I led the worship with a pack of cigarettes in my pocket and spent nights partying with drunkenness and immorality. I knew **about** God, but I had no idea what it would be like to have a personal relationship with Him. After many years of living in this cycle of sin combined with the church, I reached a point in my life where I said, "God does not exist!"

Because I had never met Him, I was tired of hearing from others their testimonies of how they met God and their lives changed. I was very tired of listening to sermons, and I said to God, "If You exist, I give You a week to prove to me that You exist. Otherwise, I will never come back to You again". And I want to tell you that God answered me in five days. After five days, a friend came to me and said, "Alex! Are you going to a seminar tomorrow? Someone will come and teach us how to make disciples and how to heal the sick".

When I heard this, I thought: "Oh, not another seminar..." But that night I could not sleep much. I felt that I must go. The next day I went and sat on the last empty chair. After about ten to twenty minutes, I felt the Holy Spirit coming over me for the first time, and I have no words to explain how I felt. I felt a warmth all over my body, and I felt love. A voice inside me said, "I am here". That was the day my life changed forever.

Today I walk in my redemption as I provoke others to stand up and have an active life sharing Jesus and His power with others. As a young man, I am determined to bring revival to this generation and beyond!

I have been crucified with Christ and I no longer live, but Christ lives in me. The life I now live in the body, I live by faith in the Son of God, who loved me and gave himself for me.

Galatians 2:20

Alexandru Iordan now lives like you read in the Book of Acts. Healing the sick and telling people about Jesus is part of his daily life. Today he is leading his own ministry. You can find him on Facebook and YouTube.

CHAPTER 5 – MIRACULOUS HEALINGS & NEAR-DEATH EXPERIENCES

◎ A Second Chance: Surviving a Severe Car Accident and Finding Faith
◎ Beyond Death and Grief: Embracing Life After Loss
◎ From Disability to Strength: How Jesus Transformed My Life

In the face of impossible odds, He breathes life where there was none and restores what was broken. These moments of divine intervention remind us that God's power transcends all human limitations, bringing life and purpose beyond the grave.

A Second Chance: Surviving a Severe Car Accident and Finding Faith

Bose experienced a profound transformation after being given a second chance at life. Raised in a church-going family, Bose attended services regularly but lived a life distant from God, indulging in parties and relationships that didn't honour Him. Everything shifted in 2000 after a severe car accident that nearly ended Bose's life, serving as a wake-up call. The accident sparked a journey towards a deeper relationship with God.

Over time, Bose learned to surrender fully to Christ, leaving behind fear, anger, and self-reliance. Now living in faith, Bose's life is a testament to God's grace and the peace that comes from following Jesus wholeheartedly.

I was once in the world, but I give glory to God for counting me worthy to be His child (1 John 3:1).

My dad passed away several years ago, and I lived with my mum and siblings from a young age. My mum would take my siblings and me to church on Sundays, and I thought attending church was a compulsory part of life. I started learning about Jesus in the children's church, but although I had an idea about the story of Jesus, I did not fully know why this was so important to me.

My mum would talk about the importance of ethical behaviour and all the things parents would generally advise their children to do to be good children and become responsible adults.

My mum was a good example, and naturally, children grow up copying the behaviour of those around them. But it was not good enough only to be good.

I got into secondary school, known as a high school in some parts of the world, and I had a lot of friends.

Upon completing my secondary education, I went to university. During this time, I realised that accepting or rejecting Jesus Christ determines how I live my life and where I spend eternity.

I had left home, as my university was a few hours' of drive from home. There, I found myself always longing to attend church on Sundays - this was normal to me growing up – as the Bible says, *"Please do not forsake the gathering of the righteous, it is important for growth"* (Hebrews 10:24-25).

I was going to church, but I still did not give my life to Christ. At that time, I attended parties and was in relationships that did not glorify God.

I was living my life like everyone else while continuing to go to church regularly. I desired God, but I did not know how to get close to Him.

Looking for God, I went for crusades, Christian fellowships, and religious gatherings alone, but I was still not a devoted child of God; something was still missing. I wished I would grow up to be a pastor, but it was just a wish at that time.

I found myself always giving my life to Christ whenever I had this opportunity but not following up to live a life of total submission to God. Though I tried to be good and felt a sense of self-righteousness, there was no quality connection with the almighty God, and I did not feel fulfilled.

Wake-up Call

The year 2000 was the beginning of my journey towards knowing God. One night, I was involved in a road traffic accident coming back from a club party.

Interestingly, I did not believe many 'men of God' in those days, especially those saying they see visions. I had been given a warning message not to attend any party in the coming weeks because, if I had attended, the outcome would not be favourable. I said okay to the man of God, but I did not listen. I said to myself - I will go to the party and then prove to my mum that vision seeing was not a thing to believe always.

I did not know what had happened immediately after the accident because I almost died. I went into a coma, and I remember waking up several hours later at the hospital with my mum and elder sister beside me. I had bandages, lots of stitches on my shaven head, a cervical collar, and severe pain.

From this experience, I learned that there is a thin line between life and death – because I would have been dead on March 11, 2000. I also realised the words from God should not be ignored, irrespective of the messenger - you either accept the message or reject it prayerfully.

During recovery, I noticed people went about their daily lives, and some would sympathize with me while it took me several months to recover. I realised that I was alone and did not need to please anyone but God. My family was incredibly supportive, especially my mum, who never blamed me for disobedience.

I realised God had given me a second chance, and I certainly did not want to misuse this opportunity.

Soon after the car accident, I fainted because I was not eating whilst being on medication, so I found myself in the hospital again. Following my recovery, I continued my journey of trying to be a Christian who had a great relationship with God.

There were lots of distractions back home in Africa. I had a good job, but somehow, I had the desire to leave the country for a while, so I travelled to the UK to study. I was studying, working, shopping and just getting on with life casually, not acknowledging God.

However, the experience of the road traffic accident in the year 2000 remained with me, and I think this made me always want to have a personal relationship with God, knowing that He gave me another chance to live right. I believed God wanted to save me.

God wants us to have a good relationship with him, but sometimes we ignore him.

I joined a church in north London sometime around 2007 and decided to join the workforce – this was when I understood how to have and nurture a good relationship with God. I served in the church as an usher, and we had several meetings - these meetings, combined with church services, listening and reading the Word of God, and desiring more of God, helped me grow in Christ.

I will not say I know the exact day I gave my life to Christ because I gave my life to Christ several times, but I still found myself living a carefree life, not acknowledging God, but what I know is that God saved me. I am now in a great relationship with my Father and Saviour.

Being a child of God does not make you immune to challenges, but you will know that through it all, God is with you, and He will bring you to your expected end, which is always good.

When I lost my sister in 2016, I wondered if God loved me, but through God's grace, I could let go. I believe my sister is in a better place.

Here are a few things I learned from my sister's passing.

1. Death is not final like most people say – It is a transition.
2. Death is part of living; if Christ tarries, we will all have to return to Him through death, so we must prepare for the other side of eternity.
3. The Holy Spirit comforts us. There will be tribulations, but they will all end in praise. Trust God.

Please do not think that God no longer loves you because you have made many mistakes. Continue on this journey to seek God. You will find Him, and you will be glad you did.

A New Life

Please view my experiences of before versus after Christ below.

Before Christ:

1. I lived in fear;
2. I did not know what tomorrow had in store for me;
3. I harboured hatred and anger towards some people;
4. I did not care about other people's feelings;
5. I would feel good taking revenge;
6. I just wanted to be a winner even if I was not doing things right;
7. I desired to fit into society at all costs;
8. I was somewhat proud and thought my achievements were my doing;
9. I made a lot of wrong decisions by myself;

10. I doubted that Jesus is real.

After I met Christ and with the help of God:

1. I no longer live in fear;
2. I live by faith and God has been faithful. I know my tomorrow will be fine;
3. I harbour no hatred and intentionally control my anger. I also continually check myself carefully to avoid entering the trap of anger;
4. I now care about people and genuinely love people;
5. I do not take revenge as I do not want to cause harm;
6. I try to live holy as God is holy;
7. I no longer strive to fit into society. Pleasing God and winning souls for Him is more important to me. He loved me first and continues to love me;

8. I now know that promotion is from God, and He provides all I need according to His riches in glory. Without Christ, I can do nothing.
9. God guides me even when I think I have made a wrong decision; all things work out for my good.
10. I have a personal relationship with the Almighty and know God is real. You need that personal relationship with God to avoid doubts.

Please give your life to Jesus Christ, feed on the Word of God, grow in this journey, and win souls to Christ. God is real, and there is absolutely no gain in sin. Start your relationship with God today and enjoy the journey. God bless you.

If we claim to be without sin, we deceive ourselves and the truth is not in us.

I John 1:8

Beyond Death and Grief: Embracing Life After Loss

Lucille's life was marked by emotional struggles, deep pain, and spiritual confusion, especially after the heartbreaking loss of her daughter. Despite searching for peace in various pursuits, nothing could fill the void. It wasn't until she encountered the love of Jesus that everything changed. Through God's grace, Lucille found healing, joy, and a renewed sense of purpose. Now, she lives with a restored spirit, sharing her testimony to inspire others to find hope in Christ, even in the midst of life's darkest moments.

My journey of faith in the Lord Jesus Christ began in 1992 when friends took me to a Spirit-filled church. There I heard for the first time that I needed to believe in Jesus Christ and receive Him as my Saviour for forgiveness from all my past wrongs so that my relationship with God the Father could be restored.

Due to my Catholic upbringing, I have always believed in God, the maker of the universe and people. Because of that connection with the church, I thought I was automatically a Christian. I believed God was up in heaven, and He is ever correcting me for my sins, and I must do different things to be accepted by Him. He was a very distant Father in heaven.

Something happened in my heart one day in that church that was quite different from what I was used to, and it completely changed the course of my life.

I had an encounter with the living God when I heard the good news that God wanted a personal relationship with me. I learned that this relationship would come through accepting salvation (forgiveness, healing, and deliverance) through Jesus, who had already paid the price so I could be reconciled to Father God. I said yes to that invitation, and a divine exchange took place at that moment. I felt an incredible peace and a sense of coming home. I felt all guilt and shame removed from my life; my burdens were removed. I felt light.

Overcoming Grief After Daughter Died

A bit about my life up to this point: when I found Jesus, I was a single parent of a beautiful special needs 8-year-old girl named Stephanie. There was a lot of guilt in having her out of wedlock. Therefore, knowing on the inside that I had been forgiven for all my past brought freedom into my life.

I have never looked back since then, but I have been pursuing to know this God and Saviour, who thought I was worth dying for because of His great love for me.

In my continued journey with the living God, I have discovered that He is a God who cares about the little things and the big things in my life and the lives of those around me. I have found that He is faithful to His promises to provide, heal, deliver, and comfort.

I had "random" acts of kindness, like having the electrical wiring of my whole house done for free just when I was figuring out the budget for it and holidays paid for even when I could pay for myself, to name a few.

In the healing arena, I have been completely healed from gynaecological-related pain that I had for over 20 years, and I stopped taking pain medication. I have prayed for other people over many years, Christians and non-Christians, and saw Jesus heal them from sciatica and other joint pains. I have also seen liver tumours decrease in size, a crooked, broken bone restored years after an injury and many more healings. I also witnessed God calming the weather so a family member could travel by sea for emergency treatment.

I have discovered He is a real God who can be trusted to do what He says He will do and that He is a God of miracles.

He is a God of comfort and hope, as I found out when my daughter died to return to her Father in heaven. It was so reassuring when I met with her Paediatrician to discuss her post-mortem results as she died peacefully in her sleep. There was no cause of death but only her diagnosis. After I told her I was a Christian, the paediatrician told me that some people just leave this life, and they (the doctors) do not know why. That was what she believed happened to Stephanie, just confirming what I knew in my heart, and so it brought comfort and hope to me to know that it was "see you later, Mum".

A little bit about the influence Stephanie had in her thirteen years on the earth: when she died, I received cards from so many people who knew her but not known to me, expressing the blessing she was in their lives: her spirituality, her smile, and how she brought joy. She was a child who could not see or speak, was entirely dependent on other people for all her daily needs and had learning difficulties through brain damage from a cardiac arrest a few days after she was born.

I discovered through her life that while your earthly tent may be damaged, your spirit is not, and the latter can still respond to God. She loved being in God's presence, worship, and prayer meetings.

I became fully aware of her connection to God after she died through her impact on the people around her. I met those people for the first time at her funeral. God became God of comfort and hope in the next few years of adjusting to life without her.

My faith grew stronger and stronger through this.

Never Too Late

How can you not love a God who loved you so much that He gave His only Son to save you? His love is unconditional, and it is the same love He puts in the heart of everyone who trusts Him, so we can all bring the message of hope and healing to everyone through love.

To that end, when I took early retirement from the National Health Service, I had time to get to know God to a higher and new level.

I completed two years at the Eastgate School of Supernatural Life. During this time, I saw my life transformed through a deeper connection with Almighty God and more profound love and compassion to see people encounter Him and His goodness for themselves. This course facilitated this as it is designed for students to know their true identity in Christ, develop intimacy with God and then impact the world around them with His love and goodness, which involves moving in the gifts of the Holy Spirit.

When you invest time and money to know God, He does not disappoint. It is life-transforming to know in your heart and mind that you are a daughter or son of the King of kings, that this makes you royalty, and that hearing from God is your birth-right. I have learned to be His daughter first and then to serve Him out of that. This brings true freedom and joy to serve Him with gladness.

As a Christian, expect God to speak to you for yourself and others. He does this in so many ways - through His Word, the Bible, vision, dreams, prophetic words, an impression in your spirit, and even through nature, to name a few.

I am still on a journey to know (understand and experience) this amazing, almighty God and Father, and this will always be the case even beyond this life.

There is victory when you follow Jesus, as He has already overcome the world and death. There is only life and light in Him. My quest and hunger to draw closer to Him grew stronger and stronger because there is no greater love to be found except the unconditional, unfailing love of God that is available to every human person on the planet.

Your best service to God will come out of that close relationship with Him, and it will be easy because it will be supernatural, as God's power enables you to do what you are here to do. This will always involve others getting blessed by what you bring from the heart of God.

You will keep in perfect peace those whose minds are steadfast, because they trust in you. Trust in the Lord forever, for the Lord, the Lord himself, is the Rock eternal.

Isaiah 26:3-4

From Disability to Strength: How Jesus Transformed My Life

Pete faced immense challenges early in life, having suffered a severe stroke at age eight that left doctors doubting his ability to talk or care for himself. Despite overcoming this, his life was filled with bullying and isolation. In his twenties, Pete appeared successful, living a lavish lifestyle as a record producer, but he still felt something was missing. The loss of his best friend, Steve, sparked deep questions about life and faith, leading Pete to explore Christianity. After attending church and having a personal encounter with God, Pete's life took a turn for the better.

I grew up as a normal child in the 1970s until I reached the age of eight, when I had a severe stroke. I was rushed to hospital, where I was put into a controlled coma due to the damage I had to the brain.

I was in that situation for over eight months. During that time, the doctors told my parents that I might not be able to talk or look after myself, meaning I may need 24-hour care.

When I woke up from the coma, I quickly understood my situation and felt let down. I locked myself away in my bedroom, not wanting to see anyone for about a month or so. It was like my life was over.

If it wasn't for my mum coming into my room one day to shake away the depression I was in, I think the doctors could have been right; I may not have been able to talk or look after myself, and I may have needed 24-hour care. I remember my mum came on that day and gave me a bit of tough love by saying, "If you cannot be bothered with yourself, then your father and I will leave you to get on with it!" Then they walked out of my room. I was shocked that if I would not have my mum and dad, who would I have?

That day my life started to change. I left my room and went out to start a fresh new life. Well, that was what I thought.

My teenage years at school were tough; as a disabled person, I did not fit in - my mum fought tooth and nail for me to be able to have a normal life. I was in the Scout movement and managed to attend a mainstream school.

All these seemed to sound good, but most of my early life, right up to the age of 30, I was bullied mentally and physically, which left me, again, totally isolated and alone.

Lavish Life

Fast forward to my mid-twenties, I am married, my job was a record producer and DJ, and my life seemed very carefree. I was living a very affluent lifestyle driving beautiful cars, living in a large house, travelling around the world, and, while away, I was staying in the best hotels. Money was never an issue.

On the outside, it looked like I had everything, but I felt something was missing throughout this time. I never seemed to be happy.

This was the moment when things started to change. My wife left me, I lost my house, and I began to hit rock bottom. It was not until my best mate Steve was taken into hospital with kidney failure that I started to think that there was more to life than what I had experienced.

One Step Closer to God

While visiting Steve in the hospital, I kept being asked by different people, "Have you ever thought of going to church?" The church was not the place I thought I needed to be.

Steve spent his final days in the hospital, and I remember the last visit I did was, for some reason, very rushed. His mum left me to say goodbye, but I think she knew something I did not know. When I said, "I'll be popping in to see you tomorrow", he looked at me with a piercing stare and shook his head. I thought this was strange but flippantly agreed with him. The following morning, I had a call from his mother saying he had passed away during the night.

Now, at that point, my world was suddenly filled with questions. How did Steve know he was going to die? Why are we on this earth? Is there more to life than just this?

I spoke at Steve's funeral, and Psalm 121 was read. It is a Psalm that I have never forgotten:

I lift up my eyes to the mountains - where does my help come from?

My help comes from the LORD, the Maker of heaven and earth.

He will not let your foot slip - he who watches over you will not slumber; indeed, he who watches over Israel will neither slumber nor sleep.

The LORD watches over you - the LORD is your shade at your right hand; the sun will not harm you by day, nor the moon by night.

The LORD will keep you from all harm - he will watch over your life; the LORD will watch over your coming and going both now and forevermore.

Again, at the funeral, someone else asked me if I had thought of going to church. This time I was thinking, 'yes, why not?' I attended a couple of churches, and I said that this was not for me; they all seemed so judgemental and did not want to listen to what I had to say.

Things changed when I went to a small church in Windlesham, Surrey. I went there with one of the people who had been asking me about God and attending church. While at this service, the lay reader called Tony was giving the sermon, and it seemed to be remarkably familiar to my life. At the end of his message, he asked the congregation, "Does this ring true to any of us? If so, please stand up".

I looked around the church, thinking, 'If I stand, will I be the only one?' I thought I did not want that to be me. Looking around, I saw several people standing, and I felt a nudge to stand up. While standing, I realised I was the only one in the church! For me, that was my first step into becoming a Christian.

I was then invited round to Tony's house, and there, for the first time, I was accepted for who I am; I did not receive any judgemental questions. I was loved!

I continued attending the church and gave my life to Christ. They found out I was a trained sound engineer, and since they needed help, I started working on the sound desk. Soon after, the bass player of the worship band, who was a member of a Christian punk rock band called "Cephas", asked me to join them as their sound guy. I started touring with them, and at some point, they asked me if I would join them in their ministry. I liked the idea, but it meant not being paid and stepping out in faith. I explained that I had only been a Christian for three months and had a mortgage, a job, etc. Then I remembered the Psalm from the funeral, so I took the step and became their full-time Sound Engineer.

Stepping Out in Faith Towards My Destiny

During the next three years, the Lord provided payment of my mortgage, I received a better car, and He provided in many other ways. While with the band, I saw many people come to faith. God was at work in many parts of our ministry.

While on tour, Andy, the bass player, had a dream – he said I would meet a lady called Cathy while we were touring. But even stranger was when he said she would wear a red T-shirt.

Over the three years with the band, we had seen a lot of answers to prayers, but this seemed impossible!

For months whenever we were playing at gigs, and I saw a lady in a red t-shirt, I would ask if her name was Cathy, but, disappointingly, it was not. I did not find my Cathy in a red T-shirt until the final year before that band disbanded, when we were asked to play a charity gig near our hometown of Camberley, Surrey. It was in a town that I had never really wanted to go to.

That town was Aldershot. That is where I met Cathy, but she was not wearing a red T-shirt. We played the gig, and I spoke with her for ages to the point the band was getting annoyed. We left, but she had impacted my life that night.

I prayed to see her again because I knew I had a full diary with Church events the next day, as I had started preaching as a lay reader at my church. But one by one, they all got cancelled. The next thing I knew, I was back at this venue for the final day of this charity gig. Cathy was there in a red T-shirt. We chatted and became close over the next few weeks. A year later, we got married, and my beautiful daughter was born the following year.

Living for God

I sit here writing this and again am looking at Psalm 121. I can see the moment I decided I wanted Christ in my life, and since then, I have never felt alone or empty, and my foot has never slipped. I found the missing piece, and that was Jesus.

I have been a Christian for over 20 years now. I now run a ministry called Alder Valley Revival, where we put together training schools about bringing "God's love into Action" by encouraging people to step out onto the streets and shine God's light and love into people's lives.

CHAPTER 6 – MENTAL HEALTH & SPIRITUAL STRUGGLES

- Loved, Forgiven, and Blessed with a Baby
- A Cry for Help Changed His Destiny
- God Spoke When He Was an Unbeliever
- God Cares About You and Your Business

Battles with the mind and spirit often feel like heavy burdens to bear, but even in the depths of our pain, God is with us. In moments of doubt and darkness, His strength sustains, and His grace carries us through. Healing begins when we surrender our fears to Him, trusting that even in our weakest moments, His love never fails.

Loved, Forgiven and Blessed with a Baby

Naledi grew up in a difficult family situation but always believed in God. After experiencing the Holy Spirit at a young age, she drifted away from her faith in adulthood, returning to a life of partying. Struggling to conceive for five years, she prayed to God, and with medical help, she gave birth to a miracle baby girl.

Her faith deepened in a small church, and a word from God revealed her husband would come to faith, which came true. Now, Naledi and her husband serve together in the worship team, living a life filled with God's peace and love.

Looking back, I can see that God has always had me in the palm of His hand and has been looking out for me.

My father was diagnosed as a paranoid schizophrenic, and my mother was an alcoholic. They were never unkind to me, but I did not come from what you would call a healthy family. God gave me a loving grandmother whom I adored and spent a lot of time with and a best friend who came into my life when I was three and is still my best friend. I spent a lot of time there, so they became my surrogate family.

I have always believed in God and attended a local Church of England church with my mum, but I did not understand who God was or Jesus. I certainly did not realise that I could have a relationship with Jesus.

One day when I was around 12, one of my friends invited me to church. It was a charismatic Bible-believing church, and as soon as I set foot in the Church, the Holy Spirit touched me, and I could not stop crying. I did not know what was happening; I knew it was that I felt peace and love.

I continued going to church until I was around 15, but then the pull of underage drinking and partying took hold, and I did not go back to church until I was 21. My life was in a bit of a mess, and I had lost my peace.

I became involved in the church and started to sing in the worship team. I made friends in the house group, but it was not long before I started getting into inappropriate relationships and returning to my party ways. I was still dipping in and out of the church. I left the worship team and the house group and began to pull away from my Christian friends. I met my now-husband at work, and eventually, we got married. He was not a Christian, but he never stopped me from going to church.

Miracle Baby Girl

I tried to get pregnant for five years, and nothing happened. We had various tests, and neither of us had anything biologically wrong. It was a mystery why we could not conceive. I was getting very depressed, and I remember saying to God, "if you bless me with a child, I will give my child back to you". I eventually got pregnant with medical intervention, and my beautiful miracle baby girl was born.

I started attending a little home church, and that is where my faith began to grow; I learned more about who Jesus was, that He loved me, that I was precious to Him, and that God was my Father and He wanted good things for me. I remember I was in the kitchen one day, and I heard God telling me that He was going to restore what the devil had taken from me. At the time, I did not understand what it meant, and I filed it away in the back of mind.

A Word from God Announced the Way

I had moved on from the little house church to another, larger church, as my daughter needed to be in Sunday school with other children, and one day we had a guest speaker come to visit us.

During his sermon, he looked directly at me and asked me to go to the front of the church. He said he had a Word from God for me and told me that I would be an influencer to my friends, particularly my husband. Two weeks later, my daughter nagged my husband to come to church, which he did, and he enjoyed it and kept coming back. He eventually committed and became a Christian.

My husband used to play bass and acoustic guitar, but he had not picked up an instrument in years. After he became a Christian, something in him made him yearn to play again. He mentioned to our pastor in conversation that he could play the guitar, and he joined the worship team.

We are both now involved in the music team, I lead worship, and my husband plays the guitar.

It is incredible what God has done for me, and He has restored what was stolen from me in my early walk with Him.

In my youth, I used to think that going out to parties was much more fun than going to church and praying, but the opposite is true. If you spend time with Jesus, just listening to His voice and letting Him guide you, it is far more interesting, fun, and fulfilling than any night out will ever be! To know God's love and peace is precious and beautiful.

Knowing that whatever storm you are going through in life, we have a big God who is there to hold you, love you, and guide you is the best feeling in the world.

"For I know the plans I have for you," declares the Lord, "plans to prosper you and not to harm you, plans to give you hope and a future. Then you will call on me and come and pray to me, and I will listen to you. You will seek me and find me when you seek me with all your heart".

Jeremiah 29:11-13

A Cry for Help Changed His Destiny

Christopher's life was marked by rebellion, addictions, and depression after his parents' divorce. At his lowest, fearing he had contracted HIV, he cried out to God for help. Miraculously, peace came over him, and his addictions vanished. He turned to church, got baptized, and committed his life to Jesus. Now healed and transformed, Christopher serves in ministry, helping others experience God's power, and is blessed with a loving family.

I grew up in a non-Christian home and did not know Jesus. At a young age, my parents got a divorce, and this affected me badly. After this, I ended up becoming rebellious and causing trouble at school. I left school with disappointing grades and failed at college.

I started work at eighteen, but unfortunately, I spent all the money I earned on alcohol and cigarettes. This started as fun but soon began to control my life. As the addictions worsened, I began to gamble and develop other unhealthy and ungodly habits.

The devil was controlling my life, but I did not know it. One time I heard voices, which made me realise the battle was real, but I still did not change. I ended up progressively getting worse and not knowing where to turn. I developed depression and had a poor self-image. I thought that nobody loved me.

At the age of 24, I made a terrible mistake, and, through a causal relationship, I thought I had caught HIV. I was scared and just wanted to run away and hide. I started to get sick and believed my life was over. In desperation, I cried out to the Lord while in the shower. I got on my knees and cried, begging for help. I said, "Lord, I know I've ignored You my whole life, but if You help me out of this mess, I promise I will follow You my whole life." As soon as I prayed, I felt all the heaviness leave and peace come into my life. I heard a voice inside saying, "Go to church, find some believers and get baptised".

I ended up doing just that, and soon after that, I noticed that I did not swear anymore - which was a miracle in itself. I did not want to smoke cigarettes or drink alcohol, I did not want to gamble, and I paid back my unauthorised debt. I left my ungodly relationship and committed to following the Lord. I was set free by Jesus Christ and given a brand new life. I also had two HIV tests, which came back clear, and I believe the Lord healed me.

I received the baptism of the Holy Spirit at the age of 25, and since that moment, I have been in Christian ministry and have seen many people healed by God's power and demons cast out. The Lord has given me a beautiful, godly wife and an amazing daughter.

Turn to God while there is still time, people. He will not let you down.

Trust in the Lord with all your heart and lean not on your own understanding; in all your ways submit to him, and he will make your paths straight.

Proverbs 3:5-6

Chris Maguire now serves as an ambassador and the UK and Ireland Overseer for John G. Lake Ministries. He is married to Margie who also serves in ministry alongside him and they have a daughter called Megan. For more information please visit www.jglm.org.uk or visit the JGLM UK Facebook page

God Spoke When He Was an Unbeliever

Steve's story is a remarkable journey from disbelief and a life steeped in sin to a profound encounter with God's transformative power. Living in the shadows of crime and rebellion, Steve was a man who prided himself on his independence, arrogance, and disregard for others. His life was marked by violence, deceit, and a deep-seated anger that drove him further away from any notion of faith. Yet, in the midst of his darkest days, Steve experienced an unexpected and powerful encounter that would change the course of his life forever. This testimony is a powerful reminder that no one is beyond the reach of God's grace and redemption, regardless of how far they've strayed.

"Go and see Alan"

It was a dark winter evening, and I was sitting in the dingy bedsit which was my home when a thought came to me. Well, it was more of an inner voice, and it consisted of just four words: "Go and see Alan."

I need to fill you in on some details at this point. Alan was a friend of mine. He was also a very strong and violent man, someone who could easily knock a person unconscious with a single punch. He was a very useful friend to have, especially given the number of enemies I had made. However, he was also a very bad person to fall out with, and recently, he had started to become frustrated with me. I owed him money, and I couldn't pay him back. As a result, I had been avoiding Alan for a while.

I responded to what I thought at the time were just my own thoughts. I remember thinking, "I'm not going to see him. I owe him money." The 'thought' just came back again: "Go and see Alan." "But he's angry," I responded. "Go and see Alan," came the thought again.

This went back and forth for around 10 to 15 minutes. There were numerous good reasons not to see Alan. In addition to what I mentioned, it would mean a 20-minute walk, and I would have to literally walk it. Not only that, but I didn't have his phone number. "What if he's not in?" I mused. None of this made the slightest difference. The thought just came back again: "Go and see Alan." Eventually, I relented and went to see him.

As it turned out, Alan was home, and he didn't even mention the money. What he did mention was a flyer he had been given, which was advertising a music event scheduled for that night. Alan explained that he couldn't go because he was taking his girlfriend out, but he kept the flyer in case he saw me (it was the type of music I was into). So off I went to this event, which was about ready to start.

On my way, I stopped off at another friend's flat to invite him. He was into Hip Hop too, so I wanted him to know about it. When I got there, he told me he had arranged to meet a group of friends that night and was about to go out but that he would bring them all along. So, with that promise, I made my way to the venue alone, expecting to see him later.

The music was pretty decent, as I recall, with the added bonus being that between tracks, the performers would share something of their personal story. All of them spoke about Jesus as if they knew Him. Normally, I ridiculed religion, but these were young people doing something I respected, so I heard them out. At the end, one of the performers got up and began to address the audience. It turned out he was the pastor of the church that put on this event. As he was speaking, something strange began to happen. It was as if God was right there, looking straight through me and could see everything—even my thoughts and feelings. I began to feel very uncomfortable.

The Depths of Sin: Violence, Deceit, and Anger

At this point, I should explain something. I was a very arrogant man, and I loved sinning. Of course, I never used the word 'sinning.' As far as I was concerned, everything I did was right. I stole and robbed, cursed, threatened, and used violence, vandalized, and vindictively swore revenge on anyone who crossed me. Furthermore, I was proud of it. I rationalized my lying and deception, and I was a god in my own eyes.

As for religion? Well, the more religious a person was, the more worthy of scathing ridicule they were, as far as I was concerned. But at this point, God was very real, and I felt as if every excuse I used was a total waste of time. That was very unusual for a man who could look at the same grey sky you were looking at and argue it was blue until I was blue in the face. My golden rule was "Never admit you are wrong... ever!"

There was one thing I could not be proud of, however, and that was my hatred for my own mum. We didn't get along, and that night I sat there listening to that man preach and heard him say, "Some of you don't even love your own mother!"

It was as if God Himself had got my number. The man continued by explaining that the whole point of Jesus' life was to die—to die for all the bad things we have done. These things separate us from God and put us under His impending judgment, but Jesus died to pay the price for everything we had done wrong.

If you think you are good enough for heaven when you die, you are fooling yourself. Nobody is. But Jesus died for our sins so that anybody who turns to Him and gives their lives to Him would be 'saved.'

A Divine Encounter: The Turning Point in Steve's Life

I rode it out. I waited for the end and hoped to just slip out the door, but before I could, a gentleman approached me and said hello. I felt deeply uncomfortable. He asked me what I thought about the message, and I said something about intending to attend the church tomorrow. His reply was, "That's good, but what if you were to die tonight? What would happen to you?" I felt more and more uneasy. I looked towards the door.

I expected my friends to arrive any minute, and here I was talking about religion to someone! Right then, it was as if God spoke to me: "You know what this man is saying is true, and you know if your friends walked in right now, you would laugh in his face and walk out."

I felt like such a hypocrite. I was caught 'bang to rights,' as they say. He introduced me to one of the members of the church who, after a brief introduction, said we simply needed to pray. I hesitated. I was embarrassed. To be honest, he pretty much dragged me into praying. I remember at that point conceding to what, for me, was a rare moment of honesty.

I said in my mind, "God, I don't know if I can live this life you're calling me to, but all I can promise is I will try." In my mind, sinning was like being on a toboggan going down a mountainside slope. It was easy and continuous. However, doing good was like walking up a mountain with a large backpack on. I realised that if I lived until I was 80, I would not make up for all the wrong I did. If heaven and hell for me were decided on the moral scale of justice, I was bankrupt anyway. So that was it. I prayed. The guy with me showed me what to pray, and I simply did the following:

- I admitted to Jesus I was a sinner.
- I asked Him to forgive all my sins.
- I asked Him to come into my life.
- I pledged to put my trust in Him and follow Him for the rest of my life.

That was it. Right then, something strange happened. It was as if a physical weight was slowly taken from my shoulders. Something I never knew was there was slowly removed. As I walked home that night, I began to notice other strange things too. My normal predilection for swearing and profanity had disappeared without any effort on my part.

My normal mindset, which was dominated by thoughts of hate, anger, and violence, had totally changed. I felt happy. I felt at peace. It was weird in a really good way. I walked home that night not really knowing what to make of it all but feeling really good nonetheless. That night, I sat on the edge of my bed and looked up at the large, sprawling collection of music I had. So much of it was hip hop music. I loved my music, and I especially loved gangsta rap. I loved the violence, the rebellion, the profanity, and the aggression. I never missed an opportunity to play my music... That is, except for that night. There was such a sense of peace in that room with me that I didn't want it to go away.

For probably the first time in my life, I passed up the chance to play my music. I didn't want that sense of peace to go away. I lay down, wondering if this really was too good to be true. I figured if this feeling was still with me in the morning, it must be real. I woke up that morning, and it was still there.

Transformed by Grace

I ended up giving away my collection of music. Alan took a lot of it. He kept asking me if this was okay. I think he thought I'd gone mad. I didn't dare tell him at the time that I had become a Christian. The day that this change happened was December 11th, 1993, and today I am still a follower of Jesus. That day is like my birthday. It was the day I became a new person. I became born again.

That was the day I gave up carrying a knife, running around in gangs, and planning how to get vengeance on my enemies. That was the day everything turned around, and I became a new person.

In over 20 years, there have been struggles. There have been good days and bad, but that one hour changed my life forever. I was on a fast track to destruction.

By rights, I should either be dead or spending the rest of my life in prison, but here I am typing this. My life is a miracle. The same God I thought didn't exist apprehended me and changed me in a single hour of one day. That was the day I started a new life.

"But God demonstrates his own love for us in this: While we were still sinners, Christ died for us."

Romans 5:8

To find out more about Steve Johnson's testimony, you can visit the website - darkness2light.me

God Cares About You and Your Business

Stephen, raised without a Christian background, faced challenges in his business until a Christian business coach prayed, resulting in a miraculous breakthrough. This led him to explore faith through an Alpha course, where he committed to Jesus. Since then, Stephen has witnessed God's power through answered prayers and miracles, including healing his stepfather. Today, he continues to see God's hand in his life and business.

I always wanted to believe in God and noticed that people who were Christians had something – they had joy; they had life in them. They had something I had not seen in other people.

My grandma was in the Salvation Army, and my mum and dad met there. They got married and did not continue in the faith. When I was young, I did not attend church or know God.

God Answers Prayers Relating to Business

In my 40s, I had a business with eight people working for me. My business was going through some difficulties because of changes the government made to the NHS.

At that time, I had a phone call from a business coach who offered me a free consultation to see if he could evaluate my business and perhaps direct me towards a more fruitful future. I had a meeting with him, and we soon became friends.

We had weekly meetings, and he helped me decide to give up the NHS work and go all private. This meant we had to buy a new property to serve the business better, be more presentable for when we had patients coming in, and be able to cater and offer excellent customer service.

We found a new building that needed to be refurbished and needed a change of use from office to industrial so that we could buy it. We made an offer subject to planning permission.

We got all the plans ready to divide it into two separate units so we could rent one and use one. I was told it would take about eight weeks to receive the planning permission.

The sellers were happy to wait, and they understood I could not buy it without the usage worked out.

I handed in my notice where I was working and went through all the applications and the design process. It got delayed many times, and I spent about £5,000 trying to get everything together. After 15 weeks, the seller was getting angry that I had not managed to exchange contracts on the building. They warned me that if I did not get it done by that Friday, they had another buyer lined up who would buy the building for a lot more than I offered, so I would lose the property.

I had a meeting with the business coach, who was a Christian guy, on a Tuesday, and he said that something or someone was preventing me from buying this property. He said, "With your permission, I would like to pray for you".

We were in the middle of the pub when he offered to pray for me. I said, "Sure, pray for me".

He thanked God for being our provider and told Him we would need an answer by Friday. He was very bold, and I remember saying that he couldn't talk to God like that, but he told me that when you pray, you should believe that you have received it, and then you shall have it.

On Thursday, I phoned the Planning Officer and asked where the planning permission was because they were supposed to call me to give me a decision. They had received too many applications, and they were understaffed. They told me that the decision would not be granted to me that week and that I would have to wait another couple of weeks. I told them I was about to lose the property I wanted to buy, which would jeopardise my business, but the woman said there was nothing further she could do.

On Friday, I was supposed to call the lawyers and the estate agents, but I could not tell them anything; I just let it go. The entire weekend I was worried and thought, 'Now I am in trouble'. The business coach called me to ask if I had got an answer, and I told him no, they did not have the chance to look at the application. He said, "Well, that is good because if this does not go ahead, it means that God has something better for you".

I did not have any faith in that answer, but on Monday, when I came into work expecting to call them, I found a letter from the Council saying that they had granted me my application, which was dated Friday. So, I did get the answer on Friday.

Because of his prayer and certainty, I could move my business forward.

Later, I did find out who was trying to prevent me from buying the property, and it was one of my staff. I trained this person, and then he went to work for another local lab. That particular guy played golf with a friend of his in the planning department, and it looked like his friend put my application to the end of the pile every week, so it never got looked at until my business coach prayed.

An Alpha Course Led to Jesus

I decided to find out more about God. I went to an Alpha course at a local church – this is a course where you have dinner with other people and you do a Bible study. You get to ask questions and fellowship with other Christians. After listening to all the testimonies in the third week, I decided that God must be true because all these people would not lie. Their stories convinced me to follow Jesus. I said the sinner's prayer and then continued to the end of the course.

Finding God was gradual for me, but since then, I have seen the power of God working in my life.

After that, this business coach got me into a good Christian church where I heard some great Bible-based teachings and saw God answering my prayers.

Hamster Brought Back to Life

I was only a year into faith when our hamster died and returned to life after I prayed.

In the morning, I saw that the hamster was dead, and my wife texted me during the day to ask me to bring a cage for the burial. When I came home at 11 pm, the hamster had been dead for the whole day. Everyone was in bed. I remember I picked up the hamster, held it in my hand, and as I walked through the kitchen, I thought I would pray. I started to pray in tongues for the hamster and saw its eyes opening. I thought, "I must've squashed it a bit", and as I continued praying, all this liquid came down my arm like it was weeing down my arm. As I looked again, it convulsed, and its body started to move. It did this three times, and then I saw it was breathing. It was not alive for long, but it was long enough for God to show me that He can bring life into a dead body. I put it back into the cage, breathing, but I did not expect it would make it through the night, and it did not.

This experience showed me that everything is possible with God. Since then, I have seen many healings.

My stepdad had prostate cancer, and the doctors told him he would need more chemotherapy if his markers went up. I asked him not to have this chemotherapy and prayed for him. I also gave him some healing teaching to help him receive the healing.

His markers went down, and he is still alive today. God did a miracle for him.

I have seen miracles in my family and in people I have met on the streets as well.

In terms of sensing the Holy Spirit, I always struggled with this; I never heard His voice in a way other people seemed to hear, but I have seen the power of God working through my life.

I had a great journey meeting different people – God is alive and He is on the Throne.

"You will receive power when the Holy Spirit comes on you; and you will be my witnesses in Jerusalem, and in all Judea and Samaria, and to the ends of the earth."

Acts 1:8

HOPE IN JESUS

If you are uncertain whether Jesus can help you, ask Him to reveal Himself to you. Many of the people who have shared their stories in this book did just that.

A close friend of mine had several specific prayers that seemed almost impossible to answer. She put her faith in God, and in His mercy, He responded to all her prayers. Here is her testimony:

"I started to question whether Jesus was alive, whether He died for my sins, whether He loves me, and if He really is the Lord and Saviour I need. Seeking answers, I came up with a plan. I told Jesus I had three things I wanted Him to do, and if He answered my prayers, I would believe He was real and follow Him.

My prayers were specific: I asked Jesus to help me secure a work contract I had been waiting for a long time, for my husband to receive a promotion, and for a friend to recover after a severe accident—he was in a coma on life support when I prayed. To make it more of a test, I told Jesus I would give Him a week to answer my prayers. Somehow, I believed He would do it.

By the following Friday, exactly one week after I prayed, God had answered all my prayers. I received my contract, my husband was promoted and took a new position, and my friend, who had been on life support, regained consciousness.

At that moment, I knew Jesus was real. I cried for joy because I couldn't believe it. I gave my life to Jesus, and a couple of months later, I was baptised. Today, I believe and trust in Him."

We live in a broken world, and it does not take long to see this. Sexual assaults, abusive relationships, drugs, stealing, and robbery are just a few of the problems we see around us.

God did not plan this. When He made the world, He created it to be beautiful and full of love, with the purpose of people being close to Him. Adam and Eve had a perfect relationship with God. We were not designed to experience pain, suffering, and the brokenness we see today, but people turned away from following God.

We are all humans, and when we experience all sorts of problems, we try to find a way out. We think partying, drugs, and alcohol will fix the problem, but they do not do anything. My friends who shared their testimonies in this book thought this, but they realised none of these 'ways out' helped.

Sometimes we get into the wrong relationships, hoping this will be the way out, but the problem is still there. Whatever you try to do to escape your situation, you find yourself back on the wheel, confronting the same problems.

God loved the world so much and suffered from seeing us pulling away from Him. Because He always longed for us to return to Him, 2,000 years ago Jesus paid the price for all the bad things people will ever do in this life. *"He himself bore our sins in His body on the cross, so that we might die to sins and live for righteousness; by His wounds, you have been healed"* – 1 Peter 2:24.

Healing is the Will of God. I experienced this myself many times. I was supposed to have my thyroid and gallbladder removed but God restored my health, and I don't have anything missing in my body.

Jesus preached a simple message. He asked us to believe in Him and follow Him - *"For God so loved the world that he gave his one and only Son, that whoever believes in him shall not perish but have eternal life"* – John 3:16.

"Repent, then, and turn to God, so that your sins may be wiped out, that times of refreshing may come from the Lord" – Acts 3:19.

If you choose to believe that Jesus died for your sins and you receive forgiveness, God promised to forgive you and invite you to have a close relationship with Him. Your spirit will get born again and live in eternal communion with God here and forever in heaven. As you do this, you become a new creation. Through the power of the Holy Spirit, God will also change you to become a better person; He will be your guide, comforter, and teacher.

"If you declare with your mouth, 'Jesus is Lord', and believe in your heart that God raised him from the dead, you will be saved. For it is with your heart that you believe and are justified, and it is with your mouth that you profess your faith and are saved" – Romans 10:9-10.

When we repent and believe in what Jesus did for us, we allow God to do what He promised: heal and restore us to his original design.

God has a good plan for your life. Believe in Him and get baptised. As a child of God, you will have His favour, protection, guidance and help to fulfil your destiny. He will also give you the authority and the power to destroy the works of the devil in your life and other people's lives.

The reality is that you are either in a close relationship with God or against God. In which of these two places are you today? Is there anything holding you back from believing that Jesus died for your sins and that He wants to help you? You can do this right now!

Take a moment and reflect on how you have lived your life and what you wish you never did. God promised He would forgive and wipe away your sins when you turn to Him. You will become a new creation, and on Judgement Day, God will not judge you based on your sins but based on the righteousness in you – Jesus Christ.

Jesus has given us all an invitation – *He said "Come to me, all you who are weary and burdened, and I will give you rest"- Matthew 11:28.*

If you are ready to give your life to Jesus, pray this prayer with me:

Father God,

I believe that out of Your infinite love You have created me. I repent of every one of my sins. Please forgive me. Thank You for sending Jesus to die for me, to save me from eternal death. I want to turn to You and to place Jesus at the centre of my heart. I surrender to Him as Lord over my whole life.

I ask You to send me the gift of the Holy Spirit so that my life is transformed.

In Jesus' name, I pray. Amen!

If you have prayed this prayer and want to follow Jesus, I would love to hear from you. Please email me at hello@carmenlascu.co.uk

Now that your spirit is born again and you have become a new creation, I recommend getting baptised (fully immersed) in water and asking a Spirit-filled believer to pray for you to receive the baptism of the Holy Spirit.

When you go down in the water, you die with Christ, and when you come up out of the water, you rise with Christ. The old life is now left behind, and the new life has just begun! Now you are ready to live a new life in Christ.

"We were therefore buried with him through baptism into death in order that, just as Christ was raised from the dead through the glory of the Father, we too may live a new life" – Romans 6:4.

Embrace a new journey as you read the Bible to discover how God sees you and who you are in Christ. You are His beloved child, you are an overcomer and you are victorious in all things through Jesus Christ who gives you strength.

If this book helped you in any way, please leave a review on the platform you bought it from and tell other people about it. If you know anyone who struggles with similar problems like anyone from this book, consider offering this person a significant gift that will change her / his life.

Hope is the blueprint of faith.

"Faith is confidence in what we hope for and assurance about what we do not see"

Hebrews 11:1.

ABOUT THE AUTHOR

Carmen Lascu studied Communication Sciences and pursued a career in Media and Marketing. After 15 years in this field, God revealed a new direction for her, calling her to use her skills to share the good news of Jesus and bring hope to others.

She is a born-again Christian whose life was transformed after receiving the baptism of the Holy Spirit and experiencing a powerful encounter with God at a Global Awakening conference. Soon after, in November 2017, she attended the Power and Love School, organised by Lifestyle Christianity in London, where she learned how to be used by God to heal the sick and deliver words of knowledge to reveal Jesus to unbelievers.

After witnessing God's work through her, there was no other path to follow but His. This book was also brought into being—led by the Holy Spirit.

Carmen is passionate about encouraging fellow believers to live a supernatural lifestyle every day, following the example of Jesus and His first disciples — proclaiming the good news and demonstrating the Kingdom of God wherever they go. She connects born-again believers and encourages them to embrace a childlike faith in the Word of God, walk in love, and step out of their comfort zone to heal the sick and share the gospel in everyday life.

As believers, we are called to bring a message of hope, love, and peace into the world. We carry the presence of God wherever we go, walking by faith and being led by the Holy Spirit. Jesus is my rock, and my foundation is built on the Word of God. The Holy Spirit empowers me to always follow His way.

ACKNOWLEDGEMENTS

I thank God for the privilege of writing this book and for connecting me with the amazing people who shared their lives with me, encouraging you to believe that there is light at the end of the tunnel.

A heartfelt thank you to my husband and daughter, for their love and unwavering support, and to my dear friend Chantal, who introduced me to Jesus, was there when I got baptized, and continually keeps me in her prayers.

I am grateful to the pastors and ministers who supported and encouraged me during my time in their churches: Andy Johnson – King's Community Church, Andy Chapman – Riverside Vineyard Church, Paul Van Essen – Greater Life Church, and Liam Parker – Flow Church.

I also extend my thanks to the ministries I have learned from: Andrew Wommack Ministries, Kenneth Copeland Ministries, Global Awakening, Lifestyle Christianity, Vineyard Institute, John G. Lake, Derek Prince, Kenneth Hagin, and many more.

Printed in Great Britain
by Amazon